Foreword by Pastor Chris Durkin

He Meets Us in the Dark

THE LOST CHAPTER

From the author of He Calls Me Redeemed

A raw, transformational journey through Psalm 88

Arman Kaymakcian

Dear Jesus,

In the empty spaces of white noise,
in the quiet static between life and death,
when everyone else left
my world hollow,
You never left the room.

I will never forget that.

With love,
Your son,
Arman

He
Meets Us
in the
Dark

Book Design and Typesetting: Enchanted Ink Publishing

The text type was set in Garamond Premier Pro

ISBN: 979-8-9892498-5-5 (E-book)
ISBN: 979-8-9892498-4-8 (Paperback)
ISBN: 979-8-9892498-3-1 (Hardcover)

First Edition

Printed in the United States of America

Thank you for your support of the author's rights.

WWW.ARMANKAYMAKCIAN.COM

I dedicate this book to my Lord and Savior,
the risen and reigning King of Kings, the Lord Jesus Christ.

No one has ever come close to loving me the way He has, and I
could never repay Him for what He has done.

I have nothing to offer except my heart, my life, and a prayer of
gratitude. That I will give willingly all my days.

And to those for whom this book was written—
who are groping to find their way through the utter darkness of the
valley, who feel as if God has abandoned them and as if morning
might never come, those tortured souls grasping for any thread of
hope and wondering if they should simply let go, who grieve, who
feel too deeply, whose memory stretches too far back in time, who
feel the sting of regret and wonder what could have been.

You are not alone. May these pages carry the hope
that redemption is possible through the final, finished work of Jesus
Christ, and that even in the darkness, even in the silence, even in
the places that feel dead,

God is still there.

"Do not say that there is no escape,
Or that you are weak with grief:
The darker the night, the brighter the stars,
The deeper the sorrow, the closer is God."

— Apollon Maykov

CONTENTS

Author's Note

If you are holding this book, I want to thank you for taking the time to read what I've written. I also would like to gently ask something of you, if I may. Please don't rush it.

This is not a book meant to be skimmed. When you see a Scripture reference, pause and look it up. Read it in context. Sit with it. Let the Word of God speak to you more deeply than my reflections ever could.

When you reach the Selah moments, stop. Reflect. Ask yourself the hard questions. Use the journaling space honestly. Don't give God polished answers. Give Him real ones. The Spirit of God often does His quietest and deepest work in those moments of stillness.

The structure of this book is intentional. It unfolds in movements, like a symphony.

Movement I carries the weight of lament.

Movement II begins to breathe with fragile hope.

Movement III rises into resurrection joy.

Along the way, you may notice that the cries of Psalm 88 begin to sound strangely familiar. The language of the psalm echoes the suffering of Christ Himself, and the "Christ in the Darkness" passages quietly trace His path through Gethsemane, the cross, the tomb, and the resurrection. This is not accidental. The same darkness the psalmist describes is the darkness Christ willingly entered so that none of us who place our faith in Him would ever have to face it alone. As Psalm 88 walks us through the deepest darkness of human sorrow, the Gospel reminds us that Christ Himself has already walked that road.

The Christian life rarely moves in straight lines. It moves in tension. In themes that return again and again, in crescendos and quiet refrains. Darkness and light, peaks and valleys often coexist. These movements are meant to reflect that rhythm.

The Christian life also includes seasons of silence. There are moments when we feel hopeless and lost, unsure of what to do with our pain. There are times when we sit in church listening to sermons filled with hope, yet feel none of it ourselves. We feel lonely, rejected, and confused. Ashamed that we even feel this way.

Christians are often told they should not worry. They should not feel depressed. They should not feel defeated. But the truth is, of course we do. Of course we walk through valleys. Scripture does not deny this reality, and neither should we.

This book is for those whose pain feels unbearable.

For those who have endured sleepless nights, tears soaking into pillows, hearts heavy with grief.

For those fighting addiction.

For those who have watched their family unravel.

For those facing loss, collapse, regret, or silence from heaven.

If you have ever asked in the dark, Am I going to make it through this night?

This book is for you.

My hope is that these pages help to draw a map through the fog. That you might read and think, I know this feeling. I've been there or I am here right now.

And more than that, I pray this devotional becomes a companion in the darkness. Not offering easy answers, but offering honesty. Presence. And the reminder that even when God feels silent, He is never absent.

FOREWORD

There are moments in life when the darkness feels overwhelming. Moments when we feel broken, lost, isolated, confused, and perhaps even abandoned by God Himself.

In those moments, questions begin to surface in the human heart.

Where is God when everything around me feels like it is falling apart?

Does He see my pain? Does He hear my prayers?

The pages of Scripture do not ignore these questions. In fact, they give voice to them. Few places in the Bible express this tension more honestly than Psalm 88.

It is here, in the cries of suffering and the persistence of faith, that this journey through Psalm 88 begins.

In this wonderful, refreshing, and honest devotional, He Meets Us in the Dark, Arman Kaymakcian reminds us of a profound biblical truth: God is light, and He is with us in dark valleys.

The Bible boldly proclaims God's holiness with absolute clarity.

1 John 1:5 declares:
"This is the message we have heard from him and proclaim to you, that God is light, and in him is no darkness at all."

This is the message of our faith: God is good.
God is only good; His goodness is without evil.
God is perfectly good; His goodness is without error.
God is eternally good; His goodness is without end.

Although this undeniable truth begs the inescapable question, "If God's holy character is unchanging and His nature is impeccable, is there any hope for unholy humanity?"

The gospel of Jesus Christ proclaims, "Yes."

Does our holy God meet His people in the darkness of this sin-soaked world?

The Word of God promises, "Yes."

Does God's Word give us wisdom in how to navigate dark valleys and endure seasons of suffering and sadness?

The Holy Spirit, our teacher, our counselor, and our comforter, guarantees, "Yes."

This is why Psalm 88 is so important, and this is why this devotional is so encouraging. When the darkness seems to surround us, not only is the Lord with us, but He has given us His Word to guide us.

The biggest book in the Bible, at its very center, is a collection of 150 psalms. The Psalms are both songs of jubilation and pleas in desperation. In fact, out of all the different genres in the book of Psalms, there are more psalms of lament than anything else.

The book of Psalms contains a total of 2,461 verses, which have guided worshipers for over 3,000 years.

The book of Psalms has 150 chapters to help us look to the Lord in every chapter of our lives.

The book of Psalms is comprised of well over 40,000 words, so whether it is a good day or a bad day, God's people might have the words to praise Him every day.

When the weight of our suffering is suffocating, and the trial surrounding us has taken our breath away, God's Word literally gives us the words to pray back to God.

The Psalms not only give us words to pray, but the Psalms also help us know how to feel. When this broken world pulls us into a black hole of sadness and anxiety, we can take what we know about God and preach it into the darkness. Not just the darkness in our world, but we can shine the Word of God into the sadness of our own hearts.

The specific psalm that this devotional is based on, Psalm 88, is shockingly honest about how hard it is when the darkness seems to envelop us.

This is why this devotional on Psalm 88 is so needed for so many Christians. Your experience is not foreign to the pages of Scripture, and your experience does not mean God has forsaken you. In fact, Psalm 88 reminds us it is the exact opposite.

As Arman beautifully writes on day 21 of this devotional,

> *"Psalm 88 carried me through the darkness, but now*
> *I was learning how to live in the light. Night after*
> *night, the flame of Scripture warmed me, and new*
> *habits began to take root. It was not out of obligation*
> *or empty religion, not out of guilt or fear, but love.*
> *Love for the One who gave His life for me."*

Amen. The good news of the gospel is that our good God sent His Son into this dark world to save us from our sin. The Light of the World took our darkness on the cross so we could have fellowship with God in the light.

1 John 1:7 continues:
"If we walk in the light, as he is in the light, we have fellowship with one another, and the blood of Jesus his Son cleanses us from all sin."

So whether it is the darkness of sin, or the darkness of depression, or the darkness of suffering, this truth does not change.

God loves you.

When Jesus died on the cross for you, it was the darkest moment in the history of the world. Yet the darkness did not win then, and the darkness will not win now.

Jesus rose from the grave on the third day, giving eternal life to all who believe. If the sadness and darkness of death could not conquer Christ, then we are more than conquerors through Him who loved us (Romans 8:37–39).

As you study Psalm 88, and as you read this powerful devotional, may the Word of God speak encouragement and hope to your soul. May you know Jesus loves you, He is with you, and no darkness can snatch you from His hands (John 10:27–30).

"You are a chosen race, a royal priesthood, a holy nation, a people for his own possession, that you may proclaim the excellencies of him who called you out of darkness into his marvelous light."
— 1 Peter 2:9 (ESV)

Pastor Chris Durkin
Colts Neck Community Church

Introduction

What if I told you there was a chapter of the Bible that pastors rarely preach from? A chapter that doesn't often get quoted or memorized. A chapter that refuses to resolve, refuses to reassure, and refuses to tie suffering into something inspirational and marketable.

It is a collection of eighteen verses that sit in Scripture like a wound that never closes. It is not likely to be placed on a plaque above the mantle in your living room or shared as a meme bathed in light on social media. I am talking about a portion of Scripture so raw, so unsanitized, so authentic, and so often ignored that some have even labeled it *the lost chapter*. I am talking about what is arguably the darkest chapter in the entirety of the Holy Bible. The chapter the Holy Spirit used to transform my entire life. I am talking about the desperate plea of Psalm 88.

It is a song and a contemplation of deep longing, agony, and despair. It does not teach us how to escape the darkness. It teaches us how to speak to God from inside of it.

The first few lines of the psalm, otherwise known as the superscription, have a lot to say about how this psalm is meant to be entered. Like all the psalms, it is a poem set to music. More specifically, it is set to *Mahalath le'annoth* (mah-HAH-lath leh-ah-NOTH; מחלָת לעַנּוֹת).

Mahalath comes from the Hebrew root *halah* (KHAH-lah; חלָה), meaning to be sick, weak, or diseased. It is the same root used elsewhere in the Hebrew Bible to describe physical illness. *Le'annoth* derives from *'anah (ah-NAH;* הְנָע), meaning to afflict, to humble, or to press down. Together, the phrase points to sickness marked by affliction.

What follows is a prayer that emerges from a body and a life under sustained collapse. The psalm signals duration through its time markers: "from my youth" (*min-ne'uray;* יְרוּעְנמ), "all day" (*kol hayyom;* סוֹיַה־לָכ), and "day and night" (*yomam valailah;* סָמוֹי הָלָיַלְו). This is clearly not a season of suffering. It is a lifelong condition.

Long before Psalm 88 was ever sung, long before its bleak words were inked on parchment or whispered in the shadowed chambers of the Temple, a story was unfolding in the soil of Israel's history. It began with rebellion, with trembling ground, with the earth cracking open beneath the feet of a man named Korah.

Korah was a Levite, a man of heritage and calling, but pride twisted his heart. He rose up against Moses and Aaron, accusing them of exalting themselves above the assembly of the Lord. The accusation was dangerous, born of entitlement rather than humility. In Numbers 16, God answered Korah's rebellion in a way that would echo for generations: the earth opened and swallowed Korah and those who followed him. It was a moment of holy judgment, a line in Israel's memory drawn with fire.

Yet in the midst of judgment, Scripture offers a small, nearly quiet sentence that becomes the seed of redemption: "*The sons of Korah did not die*" (Numbers 26:11). The ground did not take them. Grace spared them.

From this single line begins a new story, a transformation so profound that the descendants of a rebel would one day become poets, singers, and gatekeepers in the house of God.

Generations later, they were known as the Sons of Korah, a guild of musicians and guardians of sacred space, authors of some of the most beloved psalms in Scripture. They wrote, *"God is our refuge and strength"* (Psalm 46). They wrote, *"As the deer pants for flowing streams"* (Psalm 42). Their voices carried longing, trust, refuge, and praise. They did not outrun their ancestor's rebellion; rather, redemption transformed the story they inherited.

They lived at the intersection of memory and mercy. Their worship carried a weight others could not replicate, because they knew in the very marrow of their bones what it meant to stand where judgment once fell and still lift their voices in praise.

From within this redeemed family line came a man whose life would deepen the mystery of how God works through suffering. Psalm 88 is attributed to Heman the Ezrahite, a man whose name is associated with faithfulness. A detail that feels almost unbearable considering how the psalm ends.

Heman was a Levite, a descendant of Korah, and connected to the prophetic legacy of Samuel. He was known throughout Israel for wisdom. When Scripture describes the greatness of Solomon's wisdom, it does so by comparison, saying Solomon was wiser than "Ethan the Ezrahite, and Heman, and Chalcol, and Darda" (1 Kings 4:31). Heman was not only intelligent. He was renowned.

He was also a musician, one of the three chief worship leaders appointed by King David. He served alongside Asaph and Ethan. Together they shaped the spiritual life of Israel through the music of public worship, composing, instructing, and carrying the prayers of the nation into song.

Heman's family was steeped in the sacred. First Chronicles records that God blessed him with many children. Fourteen sons and three daughters served as musicians in the Temple. His household was more than a family. It was a living choir, a generational echo of worship.

Everything about Heman's life pointed to spiritual strength, communal honor, and divine favor. He was the descendant of redeemed rebels, the son of a prophetic line, the leader of worship in God's house, and a man of legendary wisdom.

So how is it that Heman is the author of the darkest psalm in all of Scripture?

Psalm 88 offers no resolution. It does not end with a declaration of praise. It closes instead with one of the most haunting lines in the biblical canon:

"Darkness is my closest friend."

That line set my heart on fire and awakened in me a desperate longing for God's salvation.

How does a man so rooted in blessing and wisdom write words that feel like total collapse? Maybe it is because those who walk most closely with God feel the weight of silence more intensely. Or maybe suffering does not discriminate at all. A glance through Scripture reveals that prophets, musicians, and kings alike all face the same storms of the human heart. Or maybe, like so many of us, he carried the deep memory of his lineage, a story that began with rebellion and judgment but was rescued by mercy. In my experience, the inheritance of grace causes a person to become even more aware of their frailty and desperation before God.

Whatever the reason, Heman gives the Church something it desperately needs. He gives us holy permission for sorrow that remains misunderstood and completely unresolved. The picturesque idealism of a perfect Christian veneer collapses when confronted with the raw authenticity in Heman's prayer.

He cries out "day and night," using the Hebrew word *tsa'aq,* a term that expresses a piercing, desperate plea. He addresses God personally, *"O Lord, God of my salvation,"* and yet no rescue comes. He prays without ceasing, even when prayer feels like shouting into emptiness. He offers his grief to God without polishing it or reshaping it to sound more faithful. He does not pretend. Like so many of us try to do.

Psalm 88 is the prayer of a man who knows God deeply but feels abandoned. It is the prayer of someone surrounded by worship yet drowning internally. It is the prayer of a soul burdened by doubt that keeps praying anyway.

And this is where the story becomes truly astonishing. God preserved this psalm. He did not soften it. He did not correct it. He did not append a triumphant ending. He preserved it. He canonized it. He invited every generation after Heman to pray this dark lament.

In the quiet hours of a psychiatric ward in a hospital in Long Branch, New Jersey, with tears carrying the weight of a lifetime of abuse, addiction, crime, death, disappointment, guilt, and shame, I did just that. With a broken voice and trembling hands, I prayed Psalm 88. And in that moment, Jesus saved me and transformed my life forever.

Heman, a descendant of redeemed rebels, shows us that ruthless honesty before God is a form of worship. The Sons of Korah show us that redemption can reshape an entire lineage. And Psalm 88 shows us that even those with deep faith can walk through darkness, dread, and doubt that feel endless.

But the story does not end in despair. It reveals a truth woven throughout Scripture: God meets us not only in our praise but also in our darkness. He hears prayers that do not resolve. He welcomes voices that tremble with grief. He receives cries that end without answers.

Heman's life teaches us that spiritual depth does not remove anguish. In many cases, it deepens it. Yet God holds a place for those who suffer.

The Sons of Korah teach us that the past does not have the final word. Redemption can transform what once seemed irredeemable.

And Psalm 88 reminds us that darkness can be spoken to God without fear and still be considered holy.

This is the story behind the psalm at the heart of my testimony. A story of rebellion and mercy. A story of wisdom and sorrow. A story of a man whose lineage was spared from judgment and whose lament was chosen by God as Scripture.

Although my own story unfolds through addiction and childhood sexual abuse, the darkness Psalm 88 describes is not limited to one kind of suffering. Grief, loss, trauma, depression, abuse, and seasons of spiritual silence all speak this same language.

I pray that God meets you here in these pages. That the Lord Jesus draws near to you in what may be the darkest and loneliest hours of your life, when prayers feel more like mourning than praise and petitions sound more like confusion than clarity. Come to Him as you are—with the weight of the world pressing you down. Cry out. Wrestle. Groan. Beg. Kick. Scream. Do what you must. God can handle it.

This is the place where transformation happens. When our souls writhe in agony yet cling to the living hope. When faith survives without answers. This is where the Lord waits to meet us.

He meets us not only in cathedrals and sanctuaries, with clean clothes and eloquent words. He meets us in stained jeans, broken whispers, filthy bathrooms, hospitals, psychiatric wards, and hidden places of misery and despair. He meets us where our hearts ache for a touch of His garment, when we feel we cannot endure another day, another hour, another minute.

He meets us wherever we are.
Whoever we are.
Whatever we have done.
Whatever's been done to us.

He Meets Us in the Dark.

A Nocturne for the Restless

(Adagio. At night. Unresolved.)

There is a fountain filled with blood
Drawn from Emmanuel's veins;
And sinners plunged beneath that flood
Lose all their guilty stains.

The dying thief rejoiced to see
That fountain in his day;
And there may I, though vile as he,
Wash all my sins away.

Dear dying Lamb, Thy precious blood
Shall never lose its power,
Till all the ransomed church of God
Be saved, to sin no more.

E'er since, by faith, I saw the stream
Thy flowing wounds supply,
Redeeming love has been my theme,
And shall be till I die.

From the hymn
"There Is a Fountain Filled with Blood"
—William Cowper, 1772

The frigid porcelain numbed my feet
as I stood in the haunted bathroom
of the psychiatric ward
at Monmouth Medical Center
in Long Branch, New Jersey.

It was 2009.

I could barely stand.
Exhausted.
Wearing a loosely tied, sour-smelling
hospital gown.

Stripped of my clothes,
my shoes, my belt,
my sense of self.

On suicide watch.

My skin pale as death.
Dark circles hung beneath my eyes.

I stared into a clouded mirror
and could not recognize
the man looking back at me.

Whatever I had been holding together
for years
had finally come undone.

Destruction rarely announces itself
all at once.

It does not arrive
with fireworks
or finality.

It is slow.
Quiet.

A steady accumulation
of small compromises,
unspoken rationalizations,
things tolerated
instead of confronted.

Over time,
they begin to press in,
bending the human soul
under their weight.

I did not wake up one morning
to find myself
suddenly lost.

I wandered there.
Slowly, but surely.

Your story may not look like mine.
You may never have stood
in a stained hospital gown
under fluorescent lights,
unsure whether you wanted to live or die.

But just about everyone I know
has tasted
some version
of darkness.

Depression.
Anxiety.
The quiet sense
that something is deeply wrong,
even when life looks functional
from the outside.

For many,
that darkness becomes familiar.

It is treated.
Managed.
Medicated.
Analyzed.

People search backward
through their childhoods,
forward through their ambitions,
sideways through pleasure
and distraction,

hoping to identify
the source
of the ache within the heart.

They fill their days with noise
and their nights with escape,
yet still feel empty.

What makes the weight heavier
is that it often comes
with a side of guilt and shame,
even when we cannot articulate why.

We are told
we shouldn't feel this way.
We are assured
that nothing is wrong.
That sin does not exist.

And yet
something deep within us
knows otherwise.

The soul carries a gravity
that cannot be explained away
by permission
or affirmation.

Standing there that morning,
I did not yet have language
for what I was feeling.

I only knew
that whatever I had been doing
to fill myself
had failed.

Whatever I had trusted
had collapsed.

The life I had constructed
could no longer hold
the weight
it was bearing.

This was not just sadness.

It was burden.

There is a difference
between suffering
that happens to us
and suffering
that accumulates within us.

Some pain is imposed.
Other pain is carried.

I was beginning to understand
that the heaviness I felt
was anything but random.

It had a history.
It had roots.

I would eventually learn
that the heaviness
I was dragging along with me
like a dead body
had a name.

That it wasn't just sadness
or circumstance
or chemistry.

That it had grown quietly
through years of choices,
rebellion,
rationalizations,
and a life left unexamined.

But standing there that morning,
I didn't yet know
how to call it
what it was.

I only knew
that whatever I had been living for
could not save me from it.

In that place,
stripped down
and exposed,
I could no longer outrun myself
or those around me.

There were no distractions left.
No illusions sturdy enough
to lean on.

Only the undeniable awareness
that I was very sick
and that I could not fix
what had brought me there.

I did not yet understand
what sin was doing to me.

But I knew,
with a clarity
that cut through the fog,
that whatever had brought me
to that mirror
could not be healed
by explanation,
effort,
or willpower
alone.

I needed rescue.

God of My Salvation, Even Here

Psalm 88:1

"O LORD, God of my salvation;
I cry out day and night before you." (ESV)

EXCERPT FROM *HE CALLS ME REDEEMED*

I began to cry like a child, unable to breathe as I let out all the years of pain and confusion. I unleashed it all upon God, thrusting it before His feet.

My knees and face on the cold hospital floor, tears and saliva dripping onto the tiles, I began to pray. "I believe, Lord! I can't do this anymore!" My voice shook. "I'm sorry, Lord! I'm so sorry! Save me! Please save me!" I cried out as if I were drowning.

REFLECTION

I can still feel the weight of desperation, even now reading this chapter of the Psalms again all these years later. There were so many nights I cried, so many nights I lived somewhere between life and death, so many nights that felt as though they might never end.

I didn't pray day and night in the traditional sense, but I did cry day and night, my heart broken, literally aching for God.

Psalm 88 doesn't open with a resolution, but simply with a cry. There is no happy ending in this verse, only a broken voice reaching upward to a God the psalmist hoped was listening.

That is where healing begins. Not in pretending you are okay, but in collapsing into the arms of a God who already knows you are not.

There is nothing you have done that He is surprised by. There is nothing you have done that He did not already die for. You do not have to fix yourself to come to Jesus, because He invites the weary directly: *"Come to me, all who labor and are heavy laden, and I will give you rest"* (Matt. 11:28, ESV).

You only need to cry out.

He is already waiting for you. He has always been there.

You do not heal yourself before you visit the emergency room, and you do not attempt to clean yourself up before you come to God. You bring the filth, the weight, the wounds and scars. You bring the pain and anguish, the broken promises, the failures, the flaws, the chaos, and the carnality. We are all level at the foot of the cross.

God will receive you wherever you are, but He loves you too much to allow you to remain there.

That is the difference between Christianity and every other religion in the world. Rather than us reaching up to God, it is God who has already reached down to us by giving His one and only Son, so that whoever believes in Him should not perish but have eternal life (John 3:16, ESV).

The very act of reaching back in faith is where transformation begins.

CHRIST IN THE DARKNESS

*"My soul is very sorrowful, even to death;
remain here and watch with me."*
—Matthew 26:38, ESV

PRAYER

God, I don't have it together. Not even close. There is so much that I
have messed up. So much that I have done that has never been spoken out loud, and so much that has been done to me. I'm not sure I
even can be saved. I know for certain I do not deserve to be. But here
I am, crying out. Please hear me God. Please save me.

In Jesus' name. Amen.

SELAH

A moment to pause and reflect

Take a breath.

Allow what you have just read to rest within you.

What stayed with you as you moved through today's reading?

Where did something resonate quietly within your own story?

How does this moment meet you right now?

If you were to speak honestly to God, what would you say?

Remain here for a while.

Let silence become part of your prayer.

DAY 2

Let My Prayer Come Before You

Psalm 88:2

"Let my prayer come before you; incline your ear to my cry!" (ESV)

EXCERPT FROM *HE CALLS ME REDEEMED*

"God, I know you're there. I've always known you're there, but I feel so alone. I need to know, really know, that you're real and that you can hear me. I need you to say something."

I opened the Bible, and in my mind, I was both daring and hoping that God would actually say something that related to my life. I opened it to a random page in the middle. The thin, almost transparent paper made a distinct crinkling sound as the pages turned that was somehow sweet to me. The page was blanketed with bold black print broken up by verse numbers.

REFLECTION

As I meditate on this verse, I picture my sons, Arman, Nikos, and Theo. I picture their small hands reaching upward, grabbing hold of me and pulling me down to their height so I can hear whatever it is they want to say, especially when they are hurting.

As a father, I want to listen. And like God, I desire to lift them up in their time of need.

I am grateful that God not only allows our cry, He welcomes it. Heman does not ask for healing or clarity at first. He simply asks to be heard.

In the middle of depression, addiction, grief, or relapse, that is often where prayer begins, with the question, "Can you hear me?"

This is not a lack of faith, but a form of it. You cry out because you still hope and believe He might be listening.

Psalm 88 shows us that even in the silence there is a sacred kind of intimacy in our reaching. It has been my experience that even though silence may endure for a season, when you open your Bible and ask God to speak, even if it is only a whisper, eventually He gives you the ability to hear.

C. S. Lewis once wrote in The Problem of Pain:
"God whispers to us in our pleasures, speaks in our conscience, but shouts in our pains. It is His megaphone to rouse a deaf world."

Perhaps this is why suffering so often becomes the place where we finally begin to listen.

You are drawing near to a loving Father. And He promises that when we draw near to Him, He will draw near to us (James 4:8).

CHRIST IN THE DARKNESS

*"And going a little farther he fell on his face and prayed,
saying, 'My Father, if it be possible, let this cup pass from
me; nevertheless, not as I will, but as you will.'"*
—Matthew 26:39, ESV

PRAYER

God, please hear me. I know I haven't prayed to You as often as I should. I don't have perfect words or polished prayers. All I have is this voice crying out to You in desperation. I have nothing to offer You except my heart. Please don't turn away. Allow my cry to come before You.

In Jesus' name, Amen.

SELAH

A moment to pause and reflect

Slow down.

Let the words settle beneath the surface of your thoughts.

Notice what rises organically.

What felt familiar today?

Where did you feel resistance or recognition?

What truth seemed to follow you after you finished reading?

What might God be inviting you to notice?

Stay present. Let reflection unfold naturally.

DAY 3

When Your Soul Is Full of Troubles

Psalm 88:3

*"For my soul is full of troubles,
and my life draws near to Sheol."* (ESV)

EXCERPT FROM *HE CALLS ME REDEEMED*

"I was locked in the prison of heroin addiction. It's a serious prison, one with gates and bars and armed guards waiting on top of watchtowers to shoot and kill any prisoner who makes an attempt at freedom. It's an institution you don't just walk out of.

Robbing my grandmother that day, though it wasn't the first time, somehow made me feel the weight of guilt like I had never felt it before. It allowed me to finally see just how depraved I had become. I was gone. There was no more of me. I was an empty shell, a house of demons, an arid wasteland, walking around in a zombielike state of hopelessness and endless agony. It was clear to me that the only way out would be death. Suicide.

Every morning, it was there as soon as I opened my eyes, hanging over me like a giant anvil. The thought that death was the only way of escaping was relentless, and I found myself thinking about it more and more. I was at the absolute lowest I had ever been."

One of the things I love most about the Psalms is the simplicity of the language. Men like King David, his son King Solomon, and the other writers who penned the Psalms had no need to use overly complicated words to provide real sustenance, because what they had was a profound ability to give voice to the various seasons of life with all their complexity. They had a supernatural grasp of depth and understanding for every human emotion we can experience in this life. The fear of abandonment, the betrayal of family, the loss of a child are all represented in words so small and so simple that they are bursting at the seams.

Psalm 88:3 is arguably one of the most honest verses in all of Scripture: my soul is full of troubles. Some of us know this feeling well. When the psalmist says his soul is full *(sābeʿāh)*, he is not exaggerating. He is saying that his soul is saturated and there is no room left to carry anything else—he is standing at the threshold of Hell. Have you been there? Have you felt that? I know I have.

And when you're trapped in what feels like a hopeless situation, when you've experienced loss, or hurt people you love, when the downward spiral feels endless, when you feel like a hollow version of yourself, it doesn't feel poetic. It feels fatal.

But this verse, as hopeless as it may sound, is still a prayer. Which means even this kind of pain can and should be spoken to God. You don't have to hide the dark parts of your story. In fact, Psalm 88 invites you to bring it forward. To say out loud, "God, this is where I am." Because healing so often begins with simply being honest with God and with yourself.

*When God puts His children into the furnace, it is
not to consume them but to refine them. He watches
closely. He never leaves the fire unattended.*
— Charles Spurgeon

Christ in the Darkness

*"And being in an agony he prayed more earnestly; and his sweat
became like great drops of blood falling down to the ground."*
—Luke 22:44, ESV

Prayer

Jesus, my soul is full of troubles. My heart feels so incredibly heavy. I've never been this far down. I feel so confused, so alone. My hope is gone, and I don't see a way out. But I'm crying out to You, because even though I'm in a pit, You are the God who reaches down to the depths. There is nothing too hard for You (Jeremiah 32:17). Please meet me here. I'm desperate for You. I'm asking You in faith.

In Jesus' name, Amen.

SELAH

A moment to pause and reflect

Pause here.

You do not need answers yet. Only presence.

What image or phrase stayed with you?

Where did your heart feel stirred?

What part of your story felt seen?

If you could respond in one honest sentence to God, what would it be?

Sit quietly and let your thoughts breathe.

DAY 4

Counted Among the Dead

Psalm 88:4–5

"I am counted among those who go down to the pit; I am a man who has no strength, like one set loose among the dead, like the slain that lie in the grave, like those whom you remember no more, for they are cut off from your hand." (ESV)

EXCERPT FROM *HE CALLS ME REDEEMED*

As usual, the second my eyes opened, a wave of hopelessness and misery swept over me, engulfing me like a flood. I lay naked in the bed, the soft white sheets cold against my skin. My mouth was dry, and I could taste the stale cigarette smoke from the night before. Subtle beams of light found their way through the venetian blinds into my dark room, reminding me that my own personal hell had only just started. The open sores across my unshaven face and forehead stung from the salt in the sweat beading up on my skin. My arms were covered in track marks from all of the injections made over the past few years—death by a thousand cuts. I lay there in agony, attempting to wrap my mind around the desperation.

At the worst moments of my life, I walked around the streets of New Jersey like a ghost. I will never forget the feeling of powerlessness and hopelessness I felt in those days. I felt as though I did not deserve to live and lived as though I were already dead.

The psalmist says, *"I am counted among those who go down to the pit."* The pit is not just a metaphor for inconvenience or mere sadness. It is one of the strongest images the Hebrew Bible uses to describe existential nearness to death and abandonment.

Heman is not just saying that he's suffering, but that he's like a walking corpse. Things like abuse, trauma, loss, and addiction do not just hurt you; they can feel as if they've already buried you. You walk around breathing, but inside you feel like a ghost.

There is no human being who has ever walked this earth who felt this as deeply as Jesus. Who better to turn to than the One who knows what it is to be counted among the dead (Isaiah 53:9; Mark 15:28)?

Maybe you've been made to feel invisible. Like your pain didn't matter. Or worse, like you didn't matter. But Psalm 88 reveals that even those who feel like they have no strength can cry out and be heard and strengthened. Being counted among the dead may feel desolate, but that is precisely the place where resurrection begins (Romans 6:4).

CHRIST IN THE DARKNESS

*"So, could you not watch with me one hour?
Watch and pray that you may not enter into temptation."*
—Matthew 26:40–41, ESV

PRAYER

Jesus, I have no strength left. I feel like I don't even exist, like I'm not really living. I'm barely surviving. People ask me how I'm doing, and I tell them I'm fine. But the truth is I've been hurting for such a long time. I'm not even sure if I can make it through this night. And while I feel invisible to the world, I believe You see me. Help me believe that I still matter, that my life means something, that I'm still alive, that You can raise the dead, including me.

In Jesus' name, Amen.

SELAH

A moment to pause and reflect

Pause quietly.

Allow today's reading to echo softly within you.

What stayed with you most from today's reading?

Where did your heart lean closer or pull away?

What might God be inviting you to notice right now?

If you were to speak honestly in prayer,

what would begin that conversation?

Remain still. Let silence do its quiet work.

JOURNAL

DAY 5

Set Loose Among the Dead

Psalm 88:5

*"Like one set loose among the dead, like the slain that
lie in the grave, like those whom you remember no
more, for they are cut off from your hand."* (ESV)

EXCERPT FROM *HE CALLS ME REDEEMED*

I didn't just overdose on the magic spell of the opium poppy coursing through my veins like waterfalls of warm water. I overdosed on the tears I had shed as sexual abuse stole my childhood, the tears God collected in a bottle (Psalm 56:8). I overdosed on the pain of my family, on the things that shouldn't be talked about. I overdosed on the pint of blood from a hundred fiends. I overdosed on the money. I overdosed on the poverty. I overdosed on the destroyed lives and shattered dreams, theirs and mine. I overdosed on everything this life and the devil had to offer me. I'd had too much of it all.

Don't bring me back. Just let me go. Let this be the last time. Let it be the needle that takes it all away.

One of the reasons this psalm resonated so deeply with me is that it conveyed a reality of pain I was living in words I did not know how to say. The Hebrew word translated *"set loose"* (*ḥofshi*, חָפְשִׁי) means to be outside protection or responsibility.

To be set loose among the dead is more than a poetic image. It is the daily reality of a life given over to grief, depression, or addiction. There comes a point where your pain begins to overflow onto those around you. Where your name is no longer spoken with love. Where your face brings grief, rather than hope. Where the world treats you as if your future has already been written.

But even in that place, Psalm 88 reminds us that God sees (Genesis 16:13). Even the ones cut off are still spoken of in prayer. Many prayed for me in rooms I knew nothing about. And if your name is being whispered in prayer, God hears those whispers. You are not alone in that grave. You are not forgotten (Isaiah 49:15–16).

CHRIST IN THE DARKNESS

"Rise, let us be going; see, my betrayer is at hand."
—Matthew 26:46, ESV

PRAYER

Father God, I've felt discarded at times, forgotten, even set loose from Your care and responsibility. But I believe that You see me, even here, even now. That You hear my voice. Please speak my name again. Let me know that I'm Yours.

In Jesus' name, Amen.

SELAH

A moment to pause and reflect

Pause gently.

Allow today's reading to settle quietly within you.

What part of the reading felt closest to your own story?

Was there something you resisted or something you longed to hold onto?

Where might God be inviting you to honesty rather than strength?

If you were to speak openly to Him right now, what would you say?

Remain still. Let silence become prayer.

In the Depths of the Pit

Psalm 88:6

*"You have put me in the depths of the pit,
in the regions dark and deep."* (ESV)

EXCERPT FROM *HE CALLS ME REDEEMED*

I should have died that day in that crack house, alone in obscurity with no one to help. I should have been a curse to my grieving family and the people I'd touched throughout the years. My mother's and father's bodies should have shaken with grief while they stood over a wooden box I'd chosen for myself. It should have held my lifeless body, a thick layer of makeup on my face, my hair combed, my hands folded. I should have grasped a set of rosary beads. Quiet conversations about what a shame it was and all I could have been should have taken place, masked by the sound of the organ at Damiano's Funeral Home in Long Branch, New Jersey. People should have knelt down one by one, hands folded. They should have pretended to pray while staring at me, making the sign of the cross they didn't understand out of sheer habit. They should have thought about how their own day would come, and then they should have eaten and drank and carried on with their lives as though I were never there.

They should have watched my body being slowly lowered into the ground while someone held my mother's hands as she screamed. They should have ordered a tombstone with some untrue epitaph to make me sound better than I was.

That's what should have happened.

REFLECTION

The psalmist in verse 6 uses language and imagery that make the depths of his sorrow unmistakably clear. He is not just in a pit but in the depths; not simply in darkness but in the darkest regions. He continues to descend line by line, the air thinning with every sentence, as though the earth itself were closing in around him.

When a person comes truly close to death, there is a loneliness and a solitude they experience that is difficult to articulate. It is like a dog going to find a quiet place alone to die. I remember, after the miraculous encounter I referenced in this excerpt, sitting in my car outside of my father's apartment on Willow Avenue in Long Branch. I had just narrowly escaped death, and as I sat there an hour later with a needle in my arm, I felt the weight of the inescapable nature of my condition. I was in a pit.

There is a terrifying honesty within the psalmist's cry: *"You have put me in the depths of the pit."*

Sometimes hitting rock bottom feels like divine punishment. But so often it is actually divine mercy. A supernatural, undeserved grace in place of the punishment we rightly deserve for the horrible choices we have made. The pit is not just a place. It is a condition. A place without escape. A place you do not just climb out of on your own.

In Scripture, the pit (*bor*, רוֹב), a Hebrew word for a cistern or dungeon, is not where God abandons us. It is where reality sets in and illusions finally collapse.

Right down the street from where I grew up in Asbury Park stood a building that was only a skeleton of what it was meant to be. For years it sat abandoned, half-built and exposed to the elements, a local joke and a quiet reminder of an intention that was never fulfilled.

Recently, I watched a video of its demolition. Engineers placed charges at precise points throughout the structure. When the explosives detonated, the building did not collapse into chaos. It folded inward, section by section, exactly as designed. They call it controlled demolition.

As I watched the structure fall, I thought about the ways God sometimes works in our lives.

What feels like everything coming apart is not always destruction. Sometimes it is a mercy wearing the face of loss.

The Lord does not always tear down in anger. Often, He dismantles carefully and intentionally, bringing down the unstable things we have built to survive, the structures never meant to carry the weight of our souls.

What looks like ruin may actually be preparation.

God makes space before He rebuilds.

And sometimes the darkness we fear is simply the dust settling before something new begins.

It is in the pit where we break open. It is in the depths where we finally look up. God does not enjoy our suffering, but He will allow whatever is needed to break our pride if it is the only thing that will save our soul. It is not always flowery, but it is honest. And honest prayers are the ones that move the very heart of God.

49

There is no pit so deep that God is not deeper still. Even in darkness,
His presence reaches us. Hope survives where God is trusted.
— Corrie ten Boom

CHRIST IN THE DARKNESS

"While he was still speaking, Judas came, one of the twelve, and with
him a great crowd with swords and clubs."
—Matthew 26:47, ESV

PRAYER

God, I don't understand why You've allowed me to fall so far. But if
this is the place where I meet You, then please let it be the beginning
and not the end. I humble myself now. Please lift me up. I need You
now more than I ever have.

In Jesus' name, Amen.

SELAH

A moment to pause and reflect

Take a slow breath.

Let the words you just read linger without rushing forward.

What emotion surfaced most strongly within you?

Did anything feel familiar, as though it had been waiting to be named?

Where do you sense God meeting you in weakness rather than perfection?

What would it look like to rest instead of striving?

Stay here for a moment longer.

Waves of Wrath

Psalm 88:7

*"Your wrath lies heavy upon me, and you
overwhelm me with all your waves."* (ESV)

EXCERPT FROM *HE CALLS ME REDEEMED*

*"I sat in my cell at Monmouth County Correctional, completely strung
out. My key bump of cocaine had morphed back into a habit of a bundle
and a half of heroin per day. I had never been in jail for more than a
few days. Honestly, though, it felt like I had been in a cell doing time all
my life. A jail cell is clean compared to the filthy spiritual prison I had
been in since I was a little boy. In a real jail, locks don't sound the same.
Real jail is nowhere near as dark, and there's always at least the hope of
getting out. In hell, there is no such hope."*

REFLECTION

Growing up in shore towns like Asbury Park and Long Branch, New
Jersey, I spent plenty of time at the beach. My father was a fisher-
man, and I spent many nights on his fifteen-foot Grady-White in
waves that felt as though they might swallow us whole. I have seen
the ocean in all its beauty and in all its fury.

I remember one day on Sixth Avenue Beach, back before there were lifeguards in Asbury Park. I was seven years old and had been in the water for hours. I had ventured a little too far out when a lack of respect for the ocean and waves that towered over my small frame gave me the scare of a lifetime. I remember the fear that overtook me as the water pulled me lower and lower beneath the surface. As panic set in, I struggled for air. The seconds felt like minutes. The more I fought, the harder it drove me under, rolling and tumbling beneath its force. I barely made it back to shore. I had swallowed massive amounts of salt water. I lay there on the sand, coughing, and gagging, my chest heaving as I tried to catch my breath. It was the closest I have ever come to drowning.

The psalmist does not say that a wave overwhelmed him, but that all of God's waves passed over him. Wrath. Judgment. Guilt. Shame. These are not merely emotions. They are floods. When they come, they engulf you.

In Jewish thought, the sea often represents chaos, danger, and forces beyond human control. To be overwhelmed by waves is to be brought face to face with powers only God can restrain.

In this verse, God's wrath is felt as unbearable weight, His waves as forces of chaos, and His overwhelming as the slow, crushing pressure of suffering that brings a person under without escape.

Have you ever felt like you were drowning in consequences? Like your past and your pain were pounding against you again and again, pulling you under without end?

It is so easy to assume that God is finished with you in those moments. That His wrath is all that is left. But the very fact that Psalm

88 is a prayer means the opposite is true. God gave us this language so that we could meet Him even in the storm. So that we would know He still hears us, even from the depths.

When Christ calls a man, He bids him come and die.
This death is not destruction but transformation. Only
through death to self does true life begin.
— Dietrich Bonhoeffer

CHRIST IN THE DARKNESS

"Then all the disciples left him and fled."
—Matthew 26:56, ESV

PRAYER

Father, the weight of everything I've done is crashing down on me. I feel like I'm drowning in shame. But if You gave me this psalm to pray, then maybe You're not done with me yet. Save me, Lord. Do not let me drown. Have mercy on me, a sinner.

In Jesus' name, Amen.

SELAH

A moment to pause and reflect

Be still.

Notice what remains after the reading ends.

Was there a sentence or image that followed you inward?

Where did your heart soften?

Where did it hesitate?

If God already understands your struggle,

what would honest prayer sound like today?

Remain present.

58

DAY 8

Shunned and Shut In

Psalm 88:8

"You have caused my companions to shun me; you have made me a horror to them. I am shut in so that I cannot escape." (ESV)

EXCERPT FROM *HE CALLS ME REDEEMED*

I was at the absolute lowest I had ever been. Almost every person who had ever loved me had distanced themselves from me. I wasn't allowed in anyone's home because I would steal anything from anyone at any given time. I had absolutely no strength left as a man. My eyes felt like they would fall out from the tears. It felt as if my soul had slipped into complete darkness. I was lost, broken, hopeless, confused, and overcome with fear, all without even the slightest hope of ever getting out of the situation I had put myself in.

REFLECTION

I can still recall the look in people's eyes when I knocked on their door, or the sound of their voice when I called on the phone. It was as if I were a walking plague. Everything about me had become repulsive to those I loved, and I knew it.

Proverbs 18:1 says, *"Whoever isolates himself seeks his own desire; he breaks out against all sound judgment."* There were times when my isolation was self-inflicted, driven by shame and a painful self-consciousness, both inward and outward. And there were other times when it was not.

There is a strange kind of grief that comes from losing the people you hold most dear, from being alive while everyone treats you like you are already dead. Maybe it is grief for the person you once were, or grief over the person you know you had the potential to be. Whatever it is, Psalm 88:8 captures that experience: a soul so ravaged by darkness that even those who once loved you begin to turn away.

I remember a day when I had called my father to come meet me, and he lied about where he was. My eyes were fixed on his van while I listened to his voice tell me he wasn't there. I will never forget the pain I felt in that moment. The pain of rejection from a father. The pain of knowing I had become a horror to those around me. The pain of knowing it was self-inflicted.

This was no longer just how I felt. It was how I was dealt with.

What began as an internal collapse eventually became public. Still, the psalmist does not stop praying. Even in total isolation, he cries out. When you are shut in and feel like there is no one left in your life to talk to, no shoulder to cry on, no way out of the darkness, believe it or not, you are in a place where God can still move on your behalf. Jesus knows better than anyone what it means to be shunned. His shoulder is forever ready for your tears. He has promised to never leave us. Lay your burdens upon Him (1 Peter 5:7).

*Do not despair when darkness surrounds you. Despair is the enemy's
voice. Hope is learned precisely where light seems absent.*
— Silouan the Athonite

CHRIST IN THE DARKNESS

*"But Jesus remained silent. And the high priest said to him, 'I adjure
you by the living God, tell us if you are the Christ, the Son of God.'"*
—Matthew 26:63, ESV

PRAYER

Father, I've felt the weight and pain of rejection, by friends, by family, even by myself. But Lord, You were rejected too. Your rejection was not self-inflicted, but You still know what this feels like. Come close to me now. I need You. My soul pants for You. Remind me that even if everyone else walks away, You never will.

In Jesus' name, Amen.

SELAH

A moment to pause and reflect

Pause here.

Allow memory to rise without running from it.

Did today's reading remind you of something unfinished or unresolved?

Where do you feel tension between

who you were and who you are becoming?

What might grace look like in that space?

Let your story be seen without making excuses for it.

Rest quietly.

Dim Eyes and Desperate Prayers

Psalm 88:9

*"My eye grows dim through sorrow. Every day I call upon you,
O LORD; I spread out my hands to you."* (ESV)

EXCERPT FROM *HE CALLS ME REDEEMED*

*It was two o'clock in the morning, and I sat in my room staring at the
New King James Bible. The golden letters on the black leather cover
reflected bits of light peeking in from the hallway. My room was dimly
lit, only by the monitors next to the bed. I began to pray.*

*"God, I know you're there. I've always known you're there, but I feel
like you're not. I need to know, really know, that you're real and that you
can hear me. I need you to say something."*

*I opened the Bible, and in my mind I was both daring and hoping
that God would actually say something that related to my life. I opened
it to a random page in the middle. The thin, almost transparent paper
made a distinct crinkling sound as the pages turned, a sound that was
somehow sweet to me. The page was blanketed with bold black print,
broken up by verse numbers.*

There are moments in life when the tears feel endless, when sorrow settles somewhere behind your eyes. It's not a matter of if we will experience this kind of grief, but when. Jesus warned that *"in this life you will have tribulation"* (John 16:33, ESV). The psalmist captures this perfectly, describing the erosion that comes from grief and tears over time. "My eye grows dim through sorrow" is not just poetry. It is the body wearing down under grief.

It is the look of someone who has cried for too long, felt too deeply, and can barely keep their head lifted. The cloudy stare of a mother or father who has just lost a child and struggles to understand why. The belligerent gaze of a person who has lost a husband or wife to death, betrayal, or divorce and feels as if life has suddenly lost its meaning. The hopeless look of a man who has woken up every day for a decade with the intention of killing his addiction, but cannot.

But still, Heman prays. Every day. That is the miracle and the movement. Even while drowning in sorrow, with nothing else to offer, he spreads his empty hands toward God.

That moment in my memoir, two in the morning, heart breaking, hands shaking over the pages of Scripture, is the living embodiment of Psalm 88:9. Even when we feel abandoned, hopeless, and alone, we cry out. And the God who gave us these words to pray is the same God who hears them.

Christ in the Darkness

"Then they spit in his face and struck him. And some slapped him, saying, 'Prophesy to us, you Christ! Who is it that struck you?'"
—Matthew 26:67–68, ESV

Prayer

Lord, my heart is heavy, and my eyes are tired of shedding tears. But I spread out my hands to You. Hear me, even in the silence. Speak to me in the dark. Let Your Word be the light I need to survive until morning.

In Jesus' name, Amen.

SELAH

A moment to pause and reflect

Slow down.

You do not need to understand everything immediately.

What questions remain after today's reading?

Where do you feel uncertainty or longing?

Can you sit with unanswered questions without losing hope?

If God meets you in mystery, how does that reshape your expectations?

Remain here for a while.

DAY 10

The Grave Question

Psalm 88:10

"Do you work wonders for the dead?
Do the departed rise up to praise you?" (ESV)

EXCERPT FROM *HE CALLS ME REDEEMED*

As I walked toward the train station, images of me jumping onto the tracks and being ripped to pieces flooded my head. The train horn shrieked not far away, eerie and echoing through my body the closer I got. I started to cry as I thought of the aftermath. My little brother standing over a closed casket. My parents forced to greet people at the funeral home, both of them wondering what they could have done differently.

REFLECTION

Psalm 88 asks a bold and terrifying question: *"Do you work wonders for the dead"*? The fear is not about God's power, but about whether the psalmist has crossed into a place where that power no longer reaches him.

It is the cry of someone standing at the edge, wondering if hope still exists beyond the grave. Not just the physical grave, but the internal one. The place where joy has died. Where purpose feels buried. Where life feels finished even though the body still breathes.

There is another place where this question echoes even louder.

The terrain of Psalm 88 begins to look hauntingly familiar when you arrive at Calvary.

The scriptures tell us that from the sixth hour until the ninth, darkness fell over the land (Matthew 27:45). Noon became night. The Son of God hung between heaven and earth, numbered with the transgressors (Isaiah 53:12). His friends stood at a distance. One had betrayed Him. Another had denied Him. Most had fled.

Then He was laid in a tomb (Matthew 27:59–60).

Silent. Still. Sealed.

If Psalm 88 asks, *"Do you work wonders for the dead?"* then Holy Saturday holds that question in its most literal form. A stone was rolled across the entrance. The body of Jesus lay in the grave. No visible triumph. No immediate reversal. Just darkness and earth and silence.

For a moment in history, it looked as though the answer might be no.

But the grave could not keep Him.

The darkness that covered the land could not hold Him. Morning broke. The stone was rolled away. The body that lay silent stood alive again.

Psalm 88 ends in darkness.

But the Gospel does not.

That moment in my story is a living embodiment of the power of the gospel of Christ. Standing minutes away from stepping onto the tracks in front of a New Jersey Transit train answers the question with a quiet but undeniable yes. God does work wonders for the dead. Jesus has full authority over life and death.

I was spiritually dead. Emotionally buried. Locked in a darkness deeper than anything I had imagined my life could reach. And still, He heard me. Still, He answered. Still, I found new life in Christ.

Maybe you are trapped in addiction, drugs, alcohol, pornography, crushed by despair or shame, and you feel the weight of being dead in your trespasses and sins. Or maybe it's grief that dug a hole in your heart. Trauma that stole your sense of safety. Depression that numbed you. Or a long season of spiritual silence that made you wonder if God still speaks.

When you are at your lowest, even flirting with the grave, remember this: the God of resurrection is not afraid of dead places. He enters them.

Christ in the Darkness

"And they stripped him and put a scarlet robe on him."
—Matthew 27:28, ESV

Prayer

Lord God, I have been closer to death than I want to admit. There have been days when I did not want to live. Please speak life into the places in me that feel buried. I believe You still work wonders. I have been sitting for so long in darkness. Help me trust You, even here.

In Jesus' name, Amen.

SELAH

A moment to pause and reflect

Take a breath and notice where you are.

You have walked through ten days of reflection.

What feels different within you?

Where has healing begun, even subtly?

Where do you still feel heavy or resistant?

Offer both gratitude and struggle without separating them.

Stay here and listen.

MOVEMENT II

INTERMEZZO: THE PEACE OF CHRIST

(Andante. Quietly. Resting.)

In that lone land of deep despair
No Sabbath's heav'nly light shall rise;
No God regard your bitter prayer,
No Saviour call you to the skies.

Now God invites; how blest the day!
How sweet the Gospel's charming sound!
Come, sinners, haste, oh, haste away,
While yet a pard'ning God is found.

Psalm 88
—Timothy Dwight,
The Psalms of David (1801)

The demons had their fun.

Tossing and turning
throughout the endless nights,
the first few weeks of rehab,

revolving in my bed,
my mind playing tricks,

dark shadows
and demonic whispers
playing some sick
and twisted game
with my soul.

I let the wooden door
close slowly behind me

as I carefully snuck
down the hallways
of Keswick Colony of Mercy
in Whiting, New Jersey.

The nausea turned my stomach,
but I loved the smell
of the charred wood
from the fireplace room.

I knelt down
in front of the tiny,
bright, glowing embers
left from the roaring fire
just a few hours earlier.

Prayers began to fall
out of my mouth,

incoherent at times,
groaning
and whimpers.

"God help me."
"I can't do this."

I stacked the wood
in larger and shorter pieces
into the tiny flames slowly,

the same way
I stacked my prayers,

some longer
and some shorter.

Carefully building
one on top of the other,

rocking back and forth,
working with my tears
and my breath

to stoke the flames
of conversation with God

from the tiny embers
of hope
that remained
within my heart.

The only thing
that seemed to give me
any reprieve
from the insomnia

as I sat
on the shiny floral-glazed loveseat
across from the fire
I had managed to build

was the fluttering sound
of the thin pages
in the red hard-covered Bible

as I skimmed
through random sections

after weeks
that felt like torture.

The withdrawal
had begun to fade.

I had fought my battle
by the grace of God.

No drugs.
No aid.
Nothing to ease the pain

except God Himself
sustaining me.

As I read,
I could not explain it,

but I felt an excitement
deep in the pit of my stomach.

Something had shifted.

I felt something
I'm not sure
I had ever felt before.

The days
when my heart lived
in agony,
hopeless
and broken,
seemed to be over.

Like Satan's icy hands
had lost their grip.

I had made it
through the proverbial night.

Through the sleeplessness.
Through the childhood sexual abuse.
Through the trauma and confusion.

Through the fights.
The robberies.
The interrogations.
The tactical narcotics raids.
The drug deals.
The holding cells and cash bails.
The crack houses.
The needles.
The funerals.
The rehabs, hospitals,
and stash spots.
The getaway cars, strip clubs,
and motel rooms.

For the first time,
maybe ever,

the fog lifted.

I smiled at God in that moment.

I had walked through hell
and was still standing.

This was hope.

This was joy.

This was submersion.

This felt like baptism.

And slowly
I began to sense

that the peace settling over me
was not something
I had created by any means.

It felt given—
a gift.

Quietly present,
almost before
I understood it.

I didn't
know what to call it yet.

I just knew
that the calm I felt
didn't come
from circumstance.

I had sat there longer
than I realized.

The room was still.

The fire burned low.

And though I could not yet
fully comprehend it,

I felt held
by a hope

that seemed to exist
outside of me,

as if it had begun
long before
I ever knelt
beside that fire.

Christ in us — the hope of glory.

DAY 11

Grace in the Grave

Psalm 88:11

*"Is your steadfast love declared in the grave,
or your faithfulness in Abaddon?"* (ESV)

EXCERPT FROM *HE CALLS ME REDEEMED*

"I had died and been resurrected, and I didn't yet understand. My heart sat in my throat, and my stomach was in a flu-like state. The anxiousness that came with the thought of arriving at a four-month rehab was beyond my full comprehension. It's not that I hadn't been to rehab before; I had been to many, but never with the intention of staying for the entirety of the program and actually changing my life. This felt different. This felt real."

REFLECTION

There are places so dark that words no longer seem to reach.

The ugly truth is that my transformation didn't come easy. It wasn't pretty. There was a lot of throw up, sweat, dirt, blood, and constipation, and a lot of crying, prayers, pain, night terrors, and demonic attacks.

Psalm 88 dares to ask whether God's love can still be spoken of from those places.

The psalmist names that place Abaddon, not just the grave but undoing itself. The place where a person is not only gone, but fears being completely erased.. Where love, even if it exists, may no longer be declared.

Abaddon (אֲבַדּוֹן) comes from the Hebrew root *ʾābad* (אָבַד), meaning to perish, to be lost, or to be completely undone beyond recovery. In the Old Testament, Abaddon names the realm of destruction itself. In Revelation 9:11, it appears again under its Greek equivalent, Apollyon, meaning destroyer, shifting from a realm to a ruler and showing how deeply the idea of annihilation runs through the biblical imagination. In Psalm 88, this word appears only once, chosen carefully, not casually, to name the terror of being erased beyond recovery.

This is not doubt about God's faithfulness. It is the terror of wondering whether faithfulness still reaches where meaning itself feels lost.

Grief is like a long valley, a winding valley
where any bend may reveal a totally new landscape.
— C. S. Lewis, A Grief Observed

CHRIST IN THE DARKNESS

"And twisting together a crown of thorns,
they put it on his head and put a reed in his right hand."
—Matthew 27:29, ESV

PRAYER

Jesus, thank You for Your sacrifice and for calling me redeemed. You see me not as I was, but as I am in You. Let Your love define me, even when the voices of the past try to haunt my memory. May my life declare Your faithfulness, especially from the places of darkness where I once walked. Let my life be for Your glory.

In Jesus' name, Amen.

SELAH

A moment to pause and reflect

Pause for a moment.

Let the weight of today's reading settle without rushing past it.

What part of this stirred discomfort or resistance?

Where did you recognize yourself most clearly?

What might God be inviting you to face rather than avoid?

If you were honest before Him right now, what would you say?

Remain still. Let silence become prayer.

DAY 12

Wonders in the Dark

Psalm 88:12

"Are your wonders known in the darkness,
or your righteousness in the land of forgetfulness?" (ESV)

EXCERPT FROM *HE CALLS ME REDEEMED*

"The darkness was overwhelming. The dark was so dark. It was endless nothingness and uncertainty. I couldn't see anything, and everything I thought I knew and trusted I now questioned.

Does my father love me? Does he know how dark it is? How scared I am? Or how hopeless and alone I feel? Will I ever get out? Can I ever get out?

I pounded on the door like my life depended on it, screaming, 'Daddy, please! Please! Open the door! Please, Daddy, don't leave me! Let me out! I'm scared! I want to get out! Save me!'

And then the door swung open. My father stood there with his arms open wide. He held me tight as I tried to catch my breath.

'Shhh, you're okay, yavrik. Calm down. Daddy's got you,' my father whispered.

'I thought you left me. I thought you forgot me.'

'Never, son. I'll never leave you, and I could never forget about you.

When you find yourself in a dark place, call out to God. He is always with you. Don't ever be afraid.'"

REFLECTION

I wrote this portion of the book about my earthly father during an experience that took place at my family's Armenian Royal Hotel in Asbury Park. But this excerpt transcends the earthly father–son relationship. What it is really about is our heavenly Father and the fear that He might leave us or forget us.

Just after I first gave my heart to the Lord Jesus Christ, I was a resident at America's oldest live-in rehabilitation center, America's Keswick Colony of Mercy. After every church service, we read the following verse together as a reminder:

"And the Lord, He is the one who goes before you.
He will be with you; He will not leave you nor forsake you.
Do not fear nor be dismayed."
— Deuteronomy 31:8 (KJV)

Throughout the Psalms, light almost always signals the presence of God. *"In your light do we see light"* (Psalm 36:9). *"The Lord is my light and my salvation"* (Psalm 27:1). Light means nearness. It means being seen and kept.

Which is what makes the darkness of Psalm 88 so unsettling. Where other psalms speak of light, this one speaks of darkness. Where others rest in the warmth of God's face, here the psalmist feels hidden from it.

In the language of Scripture, to see the face of God is to experience His favor, His nearness, His blessing (Numbers 6:25–26). To have His face hidden is to feel the terrible weight of silence, distance, and abandonment.

The absence is the point.

In the darkest places, when light seems lost and even memory feels erased, Psalm 88 dares to ask whether God's wonders can be known there. I lived that question. I screamed into the dark.

And then a door opened. Not in my imagination, but in my memory and in my spirit. God reminded me through my earthly father of a deeper truth: I have not left you.

Even in the land of forgetfulness, even in the deepest panic, even when it feels as though He is gone, God's wonders shine brightest when the darkness is deepest.

CHRIST IN THE DARKNESS

"And kneeling before him, they mocked him, saying, 'Hail, King of the Jews!'"
—Matthew 27:29, ESV

PRAYER

God, I would never say it aloud, but I admit that sometimes I question whether You are really there. But I hope and have faith that You are. Help me to see Your wonders even when I cannot see anything else. Help me trust that You are holding me.

In Jesus' name, Amen.

SELAH

A moment to pause and reflect

Breathe slowly.

Allow your thoughts to soften as you reflect.

What emotion stayed with you after reading?

Where did you sense both pain and hope together?

What truth feels difficult to accept right now?

How might God be meeting you in the middle of that tension?

Remain here a moment longer.

DAY 13

My Cry Comes Before You

Psalm 88:13

"But I, O Lord, cry to you;
in the morning my prayer comes before you." (ESV)

EXCERPT FROM *HE CALLS ME REDEEMED*

"And at that very moment, I felt a physical hug just as I had when my father opened that basement door all those years ago. Jesus held me in His arms in that room, and it was like He had always been waiting there. Though I was a grown man, I found myself to be a lost little boy, pounding on the door, my life hanging in the balance, crying out for mercy, begging to be rescued, and my heavenly Father opened the door and picked me up."

REFLECTION

Psalm 88:13 draws us into the posture of worship. *"My prayer comes before You"* is the voice of approach, of something deliberately carried into God's presence, like incense rising or an offering placed before the altar.

Heman is not describing how he feels. He is describing where his cry is offered.

I remember a night in Monmouth County Correctional when I sat awake after spending hours dope sick in a holding cell, being fingerprinted, booked, and given a jumpsuit. I was moaning in pain, starving, nauseous, exhausted, quietly crying into the mattress. It felt like an eternity. I had no idea when I'd be getting out.

There may be mornings that come only after enduring painful nights, where the only thing you have to offer God is tears. But before the day begins, before memory interprets the pain, before loneliness explains what the night has done, the prayer is brought forward and set before God. Not because the psalmist feels close, but because God has made Himself near.

Broken people like you and me can come to Jesus because God chose to dwell among us (John 1:14). Psalm 88 reminds us that prayer is not measured by its clarity or eloquence, but by the faithfulness of the God who receives it. And sometimes faith looks like waking up in the same pain and still bringing your cry before the God who hears.

CHRIST IN THE DARKNESS

"And they spit on him and took the reed and struck him on the head."
—Matthew 27:30, ESV

PRAYER

Father, I'm not always sure what to say. Sometimes I only have tears, or silence, or groans. But I believe You hear me. I believe my cry comes before You, not just once, but every morning. Help me to keep crying out and to trust that You are near.

In Jesus' name, Amen.

SELAH

A moment to pause and reflect

Pause and listen.

Notice what rose to the surface as you read.

What memory or image lingered?

Did anything challenge the story you tell yourself?

Where might grace be present even if you cannot yet see it clearly?

Speak honestly to God in your own words.

Rest in quiet.

The Silence That Shook Me

Psalm 88:14

"O Lord, why do you cast my soul away?
Why do you hide your face from me?" (ESV)

EXCERPT FROM *HE CALLS ME REDEEMED*

"I walked into your room and said, 'Dad, I'm here!' as if I had been in a race to get to you, or as if you had been counting down to the moment I arrived.

I knew you were waiting for me, but you said nothing. Not 'Hey, buddy,' or 'Inch goo nes, yavrik?' What's going on, little one?

But not this time. Your silence was a different kind of silence, beyond silent. Unending silence. The kind of silence that's so quiet it sounds like a noise. The kind that filled my heart with a terror and sadness I had never felt before."

REFLECTION

There's a particular kind of silence that unsettles the soul. Not the absence of sound, but the overwhelming presence of nothing. I know we are not supposed to admit this, but if we are honest, we have all experienced seasons in life where we feel abandoned by

God. Where we ask, God, can you hear me? Do you see me? Do you care? Do you even exist?

Many Christians find themselves in a dark season where they feel alone, ashamed, and embarrassed to speak openly about the doubt and confusion that surface during the silence of God. There is a fear of being judged by fellow believers. But every Christian who has walked with the Lord long enough knows the weight of that silence and has walked through the valley without answers, desperately longing for permission to speak authentically to God from within that pain (Psalm 23:4, ESV).

Make no mistake: as Christians, we are called the light of the world (Matthew 5:14, ESV). The darker the valley becomes, the brighter that light shines. If it feels like you are walking through hell, remember this: sometimes the Lord allows His fiercest battles not because you are strong, but because He intends to make you strong in Him. He forms warriors through weakness.

While Satan accuses (Revelation 12:10, ESV) and the trial intensifies, a loving Father watches from heaven. There are saints who will not bend, will not break, will not surrender to the darkness, but will crawl, knees scraped and bleeding, into the very presence of God. There is a type of faith that transcends circumstance, one given by the grace of God that has walked through the fire and come out on the other side without the scent of smoke (Daniel 3:27, ESV).

In Psalm 88, the psalmist asks God why He is hiding His face, why He is turning away when His presence is needed most.

That is exactly what I felt as I stood before my father. A silence so deafening it made a sound. That moment mirrored how God can sometimes seem absent, unresponsive, uncaring, or unwilling. But Psalm 88 gives us permission to speak that pain. To voice the deep sorrow and confusion when heaven goes quiet.

And yet, the very act of crying out proves that you still believe God is listening. Some might think it is a lack of spiritual maturity to pray like this. But it is actually the opposite. It takes a mature faith to continue praying from the depths when it feels futile. A faith forged in the flames.

When God seems absent, He is often closest.
He allows the soul to feel His silence so that it
may learn to seek Him with greater trust.
— St. Paisios of Mount Athos

CHRIST IN THE DARKNESS

"Then Pilate released for them Barabbas,
and having scourged Jesus, he delivered him to be crucified."
—Mark 15:15, ESV

PRAYER

Father, I don't always understand Your silence. It scares me. It hurts me. But I trust that even when You seem far, You are close. Please reveal Yourself to me again. Let me know I am not forgotten.

In Jesus' name, Amen.

SELAH

A moment to pause and reflect

Slow down.

Allow the words to echo gently within you.

What felt unresolved or unfinished?

Where do you feel longing?

What might God be inviting you to release today?

If you could ask Him one question right now, what would it be?

Remain present.

From My Youth, I've Suffered

Psalm 88:15

*"Afflicted and close to death from my youth up,
I suffer your terrors; I am helpless." (ESV)*

EXCERPT FROM *HE CALLS ME REDEEMED*

"After that day, I began to learn how to keep secrets and push them deep down into a part of me that no one would be able to see or detect, including myself, if possible. It ate me alive inside, and my life darkened.

I learned about pain, about depression, and about how to cope with it. I dragged razors across my arms to make satanic stars and other occult symbols while I watched the blood surface above my skin. I relished the pain of the cuts, always trying to feel something other than the guilt of keeping the secret and the shame of what I had done or what had been done to me."

REFLECTION

Psalm 88 is one of the few prayers in the Bible that does not end in light. And this verse, it cuts deep. *"Afflicted from my youth up."* That is a pain that does not just show up one day. It is pain that has lived with you for a very long time.

I was recently at a large Christian event my family and I attend every year called Bridgefest. It takes place in a picturesque town next to my hometown of Asbury Park and has a rich Christian history. As I sold copies of my book and talked and prayed with people, I was only blocks away from the house where I was abused. At one point, while I was looking for a parking spot, I could hear worship music being sung as I looked up at the window of that house. I was ten years old when the sexual abuse first started, long before my mind and heart could make sense of the pain I was experiencing.

The house where the abuse took place was beautiful. Just like the town itself, it looked perfect from the outside. But all those years ago, just beyond the worship and church services, was that window. And on the other side of it was the undoing of the ten-year-old me.

What began as trauma took root, spreading through years of silence and secrecy. The pain did not arrive at twenty-seven along with the heroin addiction. It was with me from my youth, shaping my identity, behavior, relationships, and even my worldview.

Psalm 88 does not exist to hide suffering. It exists so the sufferer can speak, can pour out what has long been buried. The psalmist's helplessness, my helplessness, your helplessness, and the helplessness of many others reading this is not the end of the story. It is the confession that opens the door to forgiveness and mercy.

CHRIST IN THE DARKNESS

*"And when they had mocked him, they stripped him of the robe and
put his own clothes on him and led him away to crucify him."*
—Matthew 27:31, ESV

PRAYER

Lord, I've carried things for far too long. I've buried my pain and worn many masks. But You see it all, God, and still You love me. Please heal the damage done in my youth. Meet me here, in the broken places. I trust You still want me.

SELAH

A moment to pause and reflect

Take a breath.

Let the reading settle beneath the surface.

What part of your heart responded most strongly?

Did anything bring unexpected comfort?

Where are you carrying hidden heaviness?

How might you offer that honestly to God today?

Sit quietly for a moment.

Swept Over by Wrath

Psalm 88:16

*"Your wrath has swept over me; your
dreadful assaults destroy me."* (ESV)

EXCERPT FROM *HE CALLS ME REDEEMED*

*"I should have died that day in that crack house, alone in obscurity with
no one to help. I should have been a curse to my grieving family and the
people I'd touched throughout the years.*

*My mother's and father's bodies should have shaken with grief
while they stood over a wooden box I'd chosen for myself. That's what
should have happened."*

REFLECTION

Back in 2012, the Jersey Shore was devastated by Hurricane Sandy. I
had just started a job in heavy construction installing underground
gas lines. When the storm hit, we were sent out to assess the damage in towns like Point Pleasant and Seaside Heights. Massive waves
had swept over these communities of beach houses and bungalows,
leaving them completely destroyed. I remember seeing family photos, trinkets, and random household items, the remnants of people's

lives, floating in the water and scattered across the streets, some of them partially buried under the sand.

My life was a storm, one filled with sex, crime, drugs, death, and destruction. It was like a hurricane that left only painful remnants of what my life used to be. Sometimes the weight of my past, the wreckage of addiction, shame, and failure felt like God's wrath itself. Psalm 88 does not soften the blow: "Your wrath has swept over me." It felt like I was drowning under an ocean of judgment, wave after wave breaking over my life.

During the worst part of my addiction to heroin, I had a belt that I used to tie off my arm when I shot dope. But it was not just any belt. The buckle was distinct. It bore the image of Jesus with a crown of thorns on His head and light beaming from behind Him.

I cannot tell you how many times I sat in a bathroom or an alleyway, wanting to die, a needle in my arm and Jesus' face staring up at me.

Every time I wrapped that belt around my arm, it wasn't meant as disrespect. As strange as it sounds, it was a prayer.

My words in this excerpt echo Heman's experience. What should have happened. In light of the chaos I lived in, it seemed like death was the only possible outcome.

But God.

He spared me.

When I am honest about what I deserved, and then think about the life I was saved from, I begin to understand, at least in some small measure, the cross of Jesus Christ. I realize it was not because I did anything to earn mercy, but because Jesus bore the wrath in my place. The assaults that should have destroyed me fell on Him.

The fact that I lived, that I am writing, breathing, and praying, is itself a miracle. I was swept over by wrath, but not destroyed.

Man lives not because he is righteous,
but because God is longsuffering.
— Yeznik of Kolb (5th century)

CHRIST IN THE DARKNESS

"And when they had crucified him, they divided his garments among
them by casting lots."
—Matthew 27:35, ESV

PRAYER

Jesus, I know what I deserved. I know how far gone I was. But You stepped in and took the weight. I thank You that I am still here, not because I earned it, but because You love me. Help me live every day as a witness to that mercy.

In Jesus' name, Amen.

SELAH

A moment to pause and reflect

Pause without striving.

Notice what emotions surfaced as you read.

Where did you feel seen?

What part of your story feels unfinished or fragile?

What might trust look like here, even in small ways?

Speak freely before God.

Let silence do its work.

Flooded by Despair

Psalm 88:17

*"They surround me like a flood all day long;
they close in on me together."* (ESV)

EXCERPT FROM *HE CALLS ME REDEEMED*

"It was 2009. I was twenty-six years old. There was nothing different about this particular morning. As usual, the second my eyes opened, a wave of hopelessness and misery swept over me, engulfing me like a flood.

I lay naked in the bed, the soft white sheets cold against my skin... My arms were covered in track marks from all of the injections made over the past few years, death by a thousand cuts."

REFLECTION

Flood and suffocation. Waves of sorrow closing in from all sides. I can tell you from experience that the psalmist's imagery here is exactly what depression and addiction feel like. No hope. No exit. No air.

There were so many days that began like this for me. Days when misery was waiting before my eyes even opened. Days when my eyes were already flooded with tears before I could even move. Maybe you are in that place right now. You've lost someone you love, or you're suffering through anxiety, depression, sickness, or addiction. You've cried out to God again and again, and with each cry, the silence becomes more and more deafening. That's the kind of pain and raw emotion Psalm 88 refuses to ignore, the kind of pain we've all been conditioned to pretend we're not feeling.

Looking back now, I can see that even the years before I surrendered to Christ were not wasted. Scripture tells us that the testing of faith produces steadfastness (James 1:2–4, ESV). At the time, I had very little faith to speak of. But God was already at work beneath the surface, using even my suffering to expose what I could not fix on my own. What felt like endless collapse was, in His mercy, the breaking of illusions. He did not cause my sin, but He did not waste the pain either.

And neither should we.

What is miraculous about my story is not that I escaped it quickly, but that God sustained me through all of it. Even though my journey out of the grips of Hell has been messy, Jesus never let go.

God tells us in Isaiah 43:2 (ESV), *"When you pass through the waters, I will be with you; and through the rivers, they shall not overwhelm you."*

God is not repelled by floodwaters. As a matter of fact, He walks on them. (Matt. 14:22–33, ESV)

CHRIST IN THE DARKNESS

"And about the ninth hour Jesus cried out with a loud voice,
saying, 'My God, my God, why have you forsaken me?'"
—Matthew 27:46, ESV

PRAYER

Lord, I have known the flood and the storm. I have felt waves of misery crash over me without warning. But I believe You are greater than the flood. Thank You for being with me in the waters. Help me to trust You even when I feel overwhelmed.

In Jesus' name, Amen.

SELAH

A moment to pause and reflect

Slow your breathing.

Allow the reflection to sink deeper.

What truth challenged you?

Where did you feel resistance?

What might God be inviting you to surrender?

If you were to pray without filtering your words, what would you say?

Remain still.

When Everyone Leaves

Psalm 88:18

*"You have caused my beloved and my friend to shun me;
my companions have become darkness."* (ESV)

EXCERPT FROM *HE CALLS ME REDEEMED*

"Most everyone in my life had written me off. I stole everything that wasn't tied down and some things that were. Friends, family, or perfect strangers, it didn't matter. I was an equal opportunist when it came to money for dope.

'They're gonna find me in a trunk or a dumpster somewhere,' I would tell her.

And it's a miracle they didn't. But even if they had, there was no one left in my life who wanted me around besides my mother. Everyone else had long since given up on me."

REFLECTION

Psalm 88:18 is one of the heaviest lines in all of Scripture. *"My companions have become darkness."* Some translations read, *"Darkness is my closest friend."*

In Hebrew thought, darkness is more than just the absence of light. In Genesis 1:2, before God speaks and brings order, Scripture tells us that *"darkness was over the face of the deep."* The word used there for darkness is *ḥōshek* (חֹשֶׁךְ), from the same word family behind the "darkness" named here in Psalm 88. It describes chaos. Disorder. An unformed reality. A place before meaning and structure exist. Before God's ordering word is spoken.

When the psalmist says that darkness has become his companion, he is not only describing loneliness. He is describing a life that feels undone, as if everything that once made sense has unraveled back into chaos. Before light. Before clarity. Before hope. Before salvation. That is the depth of despair Psalm 88 is willing to descend into.

This verse is not only about isolation, but about total relational collapse. The light of love, friendship, and even the felt presence of God can seem to withdraw, leaving only darkness behind. It is the grief of knowing that your presence no longer brings comfort, but concern, fear, and pain.

For me, this isolation was mostly the result of my own choices. Addiction eroded trust until there was nothing left to stand on. But this kind of abandonment is not limited to addiction. Grief can do this. Trauma can do this. Depression can do this. Chronic illness, betrayal, and prolonged suffering can slowly empty a person's life of companionship.

But when everyone else had given up on me, God never left. I did not stay buried in the dark. I prayed. I lived. The God I wasn't sure I could still cry out to heard me.

When my family and friends became like shadows and the world closed in around me, God remained. The night eventually ended. The day broke. Light returned. And I found new life in Jesus Christ.

CHRIST IN THE DARKNESS

"When Jesus had received the sour wine, he said,
'It is finished,' and he bowed his head and gave up his spirit."
—John 19:30, ESV

PRAYER

Jesus, when the world turned its back on me, You never left my side. You were there at times when no one else was. Thank You for staying with me when it felt like everyone was gone. Help me trust and believe that even when it feels like no one is there, that no one understands, that no one cares, I am never alone.

In Jesus' name, Amen.

SELAH

A moment to pause and reflect

Be still for a moment.

Let the reading settle quietly.

What question remains unanswered?

Where do you feel tension between faith and fear?

What would it mean to stay present instead of rushing forward?

Offer your honest thoughts to God.

Rest here.

JOURNAL

Turning the Key

EXCERPT FROM *HE CALLS ME REDEEMED*

"I wrote the letter in the fireplace room late that night. Then I threw the letter into the flames, watching the carefully crafted blue cursive letters, the representation of years of internal pain that had poured out of me like a flood, disappear into smoke and white ash and carry themselves up the chimney. I felt like a demon had left my body. I had been harboring this negative emotion from the time I was ten years old, and now it was gone, just like that.

When I decided to forgive, it was as if I were given the key to a master lock. I simply turned the key and opened a new chapter in my life."

REFLECTION

I can still recall the breeze coming through the window. That distinct smell that comes only between seasons in New Jersey. Chaplain Roman asking me about the abuse more directly than I cared to entertain. "What exactly did he do to you?"

The tears seeped through my ducts even as I forced the words through the lump in my throat. Memories and emotions that had lain dormant for almost twenty years quickly rose to the surface like sediment at the bottom of a lake.

Vulnerability was not easy, but from it came gratitude for the grace I had received. From that came forgiveness, and from forgiveness came the slow process of healing.

Thank God my story did not end with the repercussions of childhood sexual abuse or my drug addiction.

It did not end the way Psalm 88 ends, with darkness still pressing in. There is no sudden turn, no clean escape, no forced hope.

But the Bible does not end with this psalm. For those who keep reading, keep praying, and keep living, it becomes the ground where something deeper happens. A battleground. A victory remembered in times of trial and suffering. A foundation of faith and hope that cannot be bought or learned in a classroom. It is a faith forged in the fiery furnace of testing.

There came a moment when I stopped carrying what had already been burning me alive. The abuse and painful memories that had shattered me so many years before. Forgiveness did not erase the past or make the pain disappear, but it unlocked something. It opened the next door. Psalm 88, in its own strange way, made room for that moment.

God does not demand that we rise all at once. Sanctification is not an overnight process. He does not rush healing or force resolution. Instead, He invites us to take the next step. To open the next door. To make the next small move of faith. And when we do, God brings life from the smoke and ashes of our pain. He restores what the locusts have eaten (Joel 2:25).

Christ in the Darkness

"And Joseph took the body and wrapped it in a clean linen shroud."
—Matthew 27:59, ESV

Prayer

Jesus, I've lived with so much pain. But I want to forgive. I want to turn the key and step into what You have for me. Give me the courage to let go, the grace to trust You with the next chapter, and the peace to leave the ashes behind.

In Jesus' name, Amen.

SELAH

A moment to pause and reflect

Pause and notice.

What stayed with you most powerfully?

Where did you sense vulnerability?

What part of today's reading felt closest to your own story?

How might God be meeting you in that place?

Speak openly. Listen quietly.

The Longest Year Clean
Living a Life Beyond Psalm 88

EXCERPT FROM *HE CALLS ME REDEEMED*

"It had been a busy year since I'd gotten home from Brooklyn. It was my longest period without drugs since I was eleven years old.

I had more successes in that year than I'd had in the fifteen years prior.

So there I was, a year clean, trying to make up for a lifetime of failure, feeling happy for my friend while simultaneously wondering if I would ever have what I'd always wanted, a family of my own."

REFLECTION

Many years ago, my family's hotel in Asbury Park endured a devastating fire. So many memories and things we held dear were damaged or destroyed. I have a photo album at home that I look at from time to time, dark around the edges, burned, charred, and warped by the heat of the flames. And yet, I can still see the pictures of my family clearly.

The fire left the building mostly uninhabitable. But my family decided to construct a whole new building. What rose from the ashes was an opportunity. An entirely new structure. Beautifully renovated condos sold to wonderful tenants. My grandfather kept one of the units for himself. Over the years, my wife, my sons, and I spent many afternoons there sharing meals, conversation, and creating new memories.

What looked like destruction became the beginning of something beautiful.

Psalm 88 ends in darkness, but your story does not have to. Today marks the beginning of a new phase, the rebuilding. After years of chaos, grief, and destruction, new life is possible. A life filled with hope, beauty, and opportunity.

This is not a fairy tale transformation. There will still be difficult days. Jesus Himself warned us, *"In this world you will have tribulation"* (John 16:33, ESV). But He also followed those words with a promise: *"Take heart; I have overcome the world."*

You are alive. You are beginning to hope again.

That is often how resurrection begins. One foot in front of the other. Joy mixed with ache. Gratitude mixed with waiting.

You are standing in a place of hope, not death. And that is a miracle. Be encouraged. A new chapter has begun. The old has passed away, and the new has come (2 Corinthians 5:17, ESV).

Sometimes all you are asked to do is the next faithful thing.
Not the whole journey. Just the next step. God meets us there.
— Elisabeth Elliot

Christ in the Darkness

"And laid it in his own new tomb, which he had cut in the rock."
—Matthew 27:60, ESV

Prayer

Jesus, thank You for bringing me through the darkest places. I am not who I used to be. And though I still face challenges, heartache, and unanswered questions, I also have hope. Help me walk in the light You have given me and trust You with the days still ahead.

In Jesus' name, Amen.

SELAH

A moment to pause and reflect

Take a slow breath.

Allow the words to linger.

What felt heavy?

What felt hopeful?

Where might God be inviting you into deeper honesty?

If you could sit with Him without hiding anything,

what would you bring?

Remain still. Let silence become prayer.

Movement III

ODE TO JOY

(Allegro. Firmly. With light breaking through.)

Thine be the glory,
Risen, conquering Son;
Endless is the victory
Thou o'er death hast won.
Angels in bright raiment
Rolled the stone away,
Kept the folded grave clothes
Where Thy body lay.

Lo, Jesus meets us,
Risen from the tomb;
Lovingly He greets us,
Scatters fear and gloom;
Let His Church with gladness
Hymns of triumph sing,
For her Lord now liveth,
Death hath lost its sting.

—Edmond Budry, *"À Toi la Gloire"* (1884)
English tr. Richard Birch Hoyle (1923)

The air outside the hospital in Long Branch, New Jersey
felt familiar as I walked.

My feet moved in quick, certain steps,
almost floating above the old sidewalk,
carrying me toward the train station.

Behind me,
the film-covered windows
of the psychiatric ward
where I had died
stood only a stone's throw away.

Halfway between the hospital
and the Fine Fair grocery store,
I stopped.

To catch my breath.

Fingers resting
against a chain-link fence.

Police sirens somewhere in the distance.
The roar of a New Jersey Transit train
barreling down the tracks.

All of it faded.

Background noise.

I called out to God.

One word,
again and again.

Thank you.
Thank you.
Thank you.

Tears fell heavy like rain.

Gratitude moved through my body
like breath returning to lungs
that had forgotten how to breathe.

I was thankful for the journey.
Thankful for His faithfulness.
Thankful that my story was not over.

Most of all,
thankful that Jesus never gave up on me.

Joy did not arrive suddenly.

It came through darkness.
Through silence.
Through nights when prayer felt unanswered
and faith felt powerless.

My story was not the absence of suffering.

It was Christ within it.

Biblical joy is not fragile happiness.

It does not depend on circumstances
or disappear when sorrow comes.

Joy is not a mood.
Or a feeling.

Joy is a Person.

Jesus Christ
is the source of all joy.

He is the joy that remains
when everything else is stripped away.

The joy that walks with us through grief
without denying it.

The joy that endures
because it is rooted in resurrection.

This joy cannot be manufactured.

It is received.
Given.
Poured out.
Inherited.

Not earned.
Not deserved.

Secured by Christ.

A birthright purchased through the cross
and sealed by resurrection.

A joy that cannot be revoked
because it does not belong to circumstance.

It belongs to Him.

And therefore,
to those who belong to Him.

I grabbed a few things from the store
and hurried back toward the hospital room.

When I walked in,
my wife stood by the window.

Behind her,
the train tracks in clear view—
the place where I had almost taken my life.

She held our newborn son, Theo.

He came into this world
bathed in light.

His tiny hand
wrapped around my finger.

The love I felt overwhelmed me.

My heart too full to contain it.

It was not merely happiness.

It was joy.

Joy in the Lord.

A joy that exceeds circumstance.
A joy that fills.
A joy that holds.

A joy that remembers the darkness
but is no longer ruled by it.

The same tracks
that once called me toward death
now stood behind my family
as a testimony to life.

The same hospital
where I had died
became a place of new beginnings.

Jesus does not merely restore.

He transforms.

There was a time
when darkness felt like my closest friend.

A time when prayers were answered with silence
and hope felt buried beneath the weight of night.

I do not pretend to forget that darkness.

But it no longer holds me.

Christ does.

Where desolation once spoke,
joy now answers.

Because Jesus entered the room.

The same God I cried out to in the dark
met me there.

And the darkness
no longer has the final word.

And so I stood there,
between what had been
and what I was becoming,

staring into my son's bright blue eyes.

Gratitude rising like breath.

Thank you.
Thank you.
Thank you.

DAY 21

The Glow of New Habits
Walking in the Light Day by Day

EXCERPT FROM *HE CALLS ME REDEEMED*

"I decided since I couldn't sleep, I was going to open my Bible and start reading. So there I sat in the fireplace room, lit by the glow of the flames and the warmth of Jesus, night after night, reading whole books of the Bible, completely mesmerized, turning page after page, unable to put it down.

I prayed and asked God for rest in Jesus' name. Not only physical rest, but rest from the years of chaos that addiction brings. I began to understand the true meaning of the word peace."

REFLECTION

The Bible speaks of putting off the old and putting on the new (Colossians 3:9–10, ESV). One of the first signs of true healing is hunger. More specifically, a hunger for God, a hunger for peace, a hunger for more than just survival.

After I had experienced the love of Jesus for myself, I was no longer chasing a high. I was chasing truth.

Psalm 88 carried me through darkness, but now I was learning how to live in the light. Night after night, the flame of Scripture warmed me, and new habits began to take root. It was not out of obligation or empty religion, not out of guilt or fear, but love. Love for the One who gave His life for me.

I replaced daily rituals of habitual sin with age-old Christian disciplines. I adopted daily rhythms of reading, praying, and resting. They were not just helpful ideas or spiritual routines. They were holy ground. They did not erase my past, but they were the quiet moments with God that were shaping the man I would become.

CHRIST IN THE DARKNESS

"And rolling a great stone to the entrance of the tomb, he went away."
—Matthew 27:60, ESV

PRAYER

Jesus, thank You for meeting me in quiet places. Thank You for showing me what peace really is. Keep growing in me a desire for Your Word. Let new habits become holy habits. Let Your light guide my days, one day at a time.

In Jesus' name, Amen.

SELAH

A moment to pause and reflect

Pause.

Let today's reading rest quietly within you.

What part of the passage felt most personal?

Where did you notice tension between hope and heaviness?

What truth feels difficult but necessary right now?

If you could speak freely before God, what would you say?

Remain still. Let silence become prayer.

DAY 22

Death and Resurrection
Transformed to Transform

EXCERPT FROM *HE CALLS ME REDEEMED*

"Even if I didn't fully understand it yet, I was being transformed by the renewing of my mind. As I read, I learned more and more, and as I learned, I grew in faith.

I saw families that had been destroyed by drugs and alcohol re-united. It wasn't just an improvement on my old self. It was a complete death and resurrection to new life in Jesus Christ."

REFLECTION

My younger brother Raphi recently sent me letters we had written to each other when I was about one month into my four-month stay in rehab. Reading them now, what became obvious was the shift that was taking place mentally, spiritually, and emotionally. You can see it in my words, my attitude, my outlook. What I hadn't been able to do in a lifetime, God did in a matter of weeks. In one month's time, I was unrecognizable.

Resurrection happened for me in one dramatic moment. But sanctification showed up more quietly. My mind changed over weeks and months. My heart softened. My faith grew over time.

Every morning I woke up with hope and purpose. It became clear this wasn't just an improved version of my old life. It was a different life altogether.

This is what God does. He doesn't reform the old self. He brings forth new life. And that life begins to transform everything it touches. I didn't recognize it all at once. I was learning. I was listening. I was being renewed in ways I couldn't yet comprehend. And as that renewal took place, something unexpected happened. It didn't stop with me.

I began to see families restored through the power of prayer. Lives rebuilt. Chains that once felt unbreakable loosened and fell away. Not because anyone was trying harder, but because Christ was doing something entirely new.

He became what we are that He might make us what He is.
— Athanasius of Alexandria

CHRIST IN THE DARKNESS

"But on the first day of the week, at early dawn, they went to the tomb."
—Luke 24:1, ESV

PRAYER

Jesus, thank You for not just helping me cope, but raising me to new life. Thank You for transforming me from the inside out. Keep growing me. Use my story to bring hope and healing to others.

In Jesus' name, Amen.

SELAH

A moment to pause and reflect

Slow down.

Allow the words to echo without forcing understanding.

What emotion surfaced unexpectedly?

Where do you feel unseen or misunderstood?

What might it look like to bring that honestly before God?

Sit quietly and listen.

A Story Shared to Save
From Wreckage to Witness

EXCERPT FROM *HE CALLS ME REDEEMED*

"I'd love it if you turned toward God, turned away from evil, and were saved, and if my story was somehow a part of your story, I'd love that too.

And I'd love to see you one day and break bread with you in heaven a million miles away from pain, from tears, from fears, and from loss. That is my prayer, in Jesus' name, amen."

REFLECTION

I wish I could say that all it took was a prayer in a psychiatric ward and a subsequent four-month Christian rehabilitation program to mend all that had been torn apart in my life. The truth is, there were many ups and downs. Peaks and valleys. Spiritual learning curves. Even after all the messiness and more self-inflicted pain, after time and tears and prayers, something had shifted in my walk with Jesus, as I hope and pray it is now shifting in you. Healing was no longer just about surviving. A quiet calling was beginning to take shape.

And as I persevered, although I was often unsure and still fragile and unfaithful, I experienced the sustaining grace of God. Grace that did not rush me out of the process, but met me in it and carried me forward.

I did the only reasonable thing I could do. I told everyone and anyone who would listen what Jesus Christ had done in my life. I did not share my story because I had answers to life's most difficult questions. I did not share it because I had somehow figured everything out. I shared it simply because I had been miraculously transformed. Jesus had saved my life, and I could not keep it to myself anymore. What God had done felt too costly, too sacred, too personal to stay private.

That prayer in this excerpt came from a simple place. I wanted to give glory to the One who had healed me and made me whole. I wanted others to know the same mercy and love I had received. I wanted them to turn toward God, to step out of the wreckage, and to find life. Not someday. Not after one more hit. Not tomorrow, or when they hit bottom, but now.

The grace of God doesn't end with the one who receives it. It reaches outward. It becomes a cup that overflows, pouring out into all those around you. It doesn't just feed you. It invites others to the table as well. And somehow, God uses what was once broken in us to help restore and lead someone else who is lost back home.

CHRIST IN THE DARKNESS

*"Why do you seek the living among the dead?
He is not here, but has risen."*
—Luke 24:5–6, ESV

PRAYER

Jesus, thank You for trusting me with a story to share. A testimony to proclaim. Let my words be light to those in the dark. Let my wounds become witness. Let every part of what You have redeemed in me point someone else home to You.

In Jesus' name, Amen.

SELAH

A moment to pause and reflect

Take a breath.

Notice what resonated with you after reading.

What part of your story mirrors today's reflection?

Where did you feel either fragility or strength?

How might God desire to use you for His glory?

Rest here a moment.

DAY 24

Living From Who He Says You Are
Redeemed Identity

EXCERPT FROM *HE CALLS ME REDEEMED*

"It has been in my deepest failures, weaknesses, and pain that I've found strength in Jesus, the one who defeated death itself when He rose up three days after they killed Him, neatly folded the clothes He had been buried in, rolled away the enormous stone with which they'd sealed the tomb, and walked out of His own grave."

"It didn't matter that I had fallen again. I wasn't who the world thought I was or even who I thought I was. I was exactly who my Father said I was.

And just like a father picks his child up when he stumbles and falls, Jesus picked me up and set my feet back on the ground."

REFLECTION

Even after walking with Jesus for years, there are times we wander. Times when we are foolish enough to return to our own vomit (Prov. 26:11, ESV). Times when we fall. But thank God the truth of your identity in Christ does not rest on your perfection. It rests on His. If you are in Christ and you have given your life to Him, He calls you beloved.

The context of this excerpt is that even after all the Lord had done in my life, I had given in to temptation and found myself right back where I started. But there was one significant difference. I had the Holy Spirit's power living inside of me. My story of grace in the midst of my own sin and failure stands as a testament to God's faithfulness and loving-kindness. God's mercy doesn't bury us under the weight of condemnation. Instead, it lifts us above our failures. It reminds us that salvation doesn't consist of one clean moment. It is the continual fulfillment of the promise of our hope in Christ alone. Philippians 2:12 tells us to work out our salvation with fear and trembling.

You aren't merely who the world declares you to be. You aren't the sum of your lowest moments or the heights of your successes. You are who your Father says you are. And if you have put your trust and faith in Him and repented of your sin, He calls you His own. He calls you beloved. He calls you redeemed.

So when you stumble, and you will, don't retreat into shame. Don't isolate yourself and play into the devil's hands. As my pastor, Chris Durkin, has often said, "When the devil reminds you of your past, remind him of his future." Let Jesus pick you up and help you begin again. That is what grace does. It convicts. It corrects. It restores. Every time.

Do not be surprised if you fall every day.
Do not give up, but stand your ground courageously.
— John Climacus

CHRIST IN THE DARKNESS

"He is not here, for he has risen, as he said."
—Matthew 28:6, ESV

PRAYER

Father, thank You for calling me by name even when I fall. Help me believe what You say about me. Pick me up again today. Let me walk in the truth that I am Yours, fully known and fully loved.

In Jesus' name, Amen.

SELAH

A moment to pause and reflect

Pause without rushing.

Let the words settle beneath the surface.

What challenged you?

What comforted you?

Where might God be inviting you to remain instead of escape?

Speak honestly. Listen carefully.

DAY 25

Joy Returns with Jesus
Laughter, Light, and Life Again

EXCERPT FROM *HE CALLS ME REDEEMED*

"Prior to me being saved, there had been nothing particularly funny about my life. But during those months at Keswick, I found myself laughing out loud for the first time in a long time and enjoying things like the sunset as if I had never seen one before.

I became more than friends with the guys in the colony. We were all part of God's family. We were brothers. We prayed together, sang together, worshiped together, ate together, and laughed and cried together. It wasn't just an improvement on my old self. It was a complete death and resurrection to new life in Jesus Christ."

REFLECTION

I will never forget the sunsets, sitting on the wooden table at the edge of the lake at Keswick Colony of Mercy. Strange, nameless colors seemed to converge like some divine oil on canvas. It was as if I had never seen a sunset before. It was like pain in reverse. That is the only way I know how to describe it.

I had seen countless sunsets on the Jersey Shore, but I had never seen colors that vivid. Not until after I was saved. It was as if I had never truly seen one at all.

One of the clearest signs that God is restoring a soul is the return of joy. Joy is not fragile happiness. It is something deeper. In the New Testament, the word for joy, *chara* (χαρά), belongs to the same word family as *charis* (χάρις), grace. Joy grows where grace has taken root.

Not forced happiness. Not performance. But real happiness regardless of circumstance. Laughter that rises from the ashes of mourning.

In this season of my life, I didn't just survive. I belonged. I found fellowship. I learned how to sing again, eat together again, laugh again. That was new life in Christ. That was the light of the gospel breaking through my brokenness.

God didn't just redeem my pain. He returned things I had forgotten existed. Things like sunsets, brotherhood, and laughter. Because He isn't only a rescuer. He is a restorer.

Joy is the serious business of Heaven.
— C. S. Lewis

CHRIST IN THE DARKNESS

"Jesus said to her, 'Mary.'
She turned and said to him in Aramaic, 'Rabboni!'"
—John 20:16, ESV

PRAYER

Jesus, thank You for joy. Thank You for the brothers and sisters who walk this road with me. Thank You for turning my tears into laughter. Keep restoring what I thought I lost, day by day, laugh by laugh.

In Jesus' name, Amen.

SELAH

A moment to pause and reflect

Be still.

Allow the reading to unfold slowly within you.

What felt unresolved?

Where do you sense longing?

What part of your heart feels tired?

What are some ways to lay that down before God today?

Remain here a while.

JOURNAL

In This Place: Peace
Learning to Dwell, Not Run

Excerpt from *He Calls Me Redeemed*

"We pulled into the driveway, passing the small white chapel where I'd attended the original Bible studies that had set this all in motion, and a rugged wooden cross standing firmly next to a sign that read Colony of Mercy, 'In this place I will give thee peace.'

Peace. I didn't know the meaning of the word. Maybe I never had."

Reflection

I remember how still the forest was at rehab during my first few days of life with Jesus. I remember being horrified by the sound of silence, standing alone with nothing but time to be present with everything I was feeling.

Sometimes God brings us full circle, not to haunt us, but to heal us. Places that were once unfamiliar, or even uncomfortable can become holy ground.

I did not truly know peace before I came to Christ. Maybe after so many years of chaos, I feared it. I may have doubted it was even real. I've heard it said that escapism is the preferred drug of the weary soul. Silence and stillness can be excruciating for a person who has endured almost constant trauma from their earliest years. But Jesus waits for us there. In quiet places. In remembered grace. In moments where we finally stop running long enough to feel.

This is what walking with God becomes. The past is not erased, but redeemed. Places we once wanted to flee from become places we are able to return to without fear.

Peace is not a feeling. It is a Person. And He meets us as much in the darkness as He does in the light.

In John 15, Jesus says, *"Abide in me, and I in you."* The word Jesus uses for "abide" is the Greek *menō,* which means to remain, to stay, to dwell, to continue, to make one's home. Peace grows when we remain. When we dwell. When we stay rooted instead of running. Nothing about the place itself is magic. But when we abide, when we make our home with Christ, He is faithful to meet us.

CHRIST IN THE DARKNESS

*"When he had said this, he showed them his hands and his side.
Then the disciples were glad when they saw the Lord."*
—John 20:20, ESV

PRAYER

Jesus, thank You for bringing me back to the place where peace first found me. Teach me to dwell, not just physically, but spiritually. Let my life be planted in the peace You promised.

In Jesus' name, Amen.

SELAH

A moment to pause and reflect

Slow breaths now.

You've made it through so much.

Let the reflection settle deeper.

What are you grateful for?

What ways can you express gratitude to God?

What would honesty with God look like in this moment?

Offer your thoughts without holding back.

DAY 27

Faithfulness in the Filth

EXCERPT FROM *HE CALLS ME REDEEMED*

"My job was to clean up around the colony: emptying garbage cans, vacuuming, sweeping floors, cleaning windows. I hadn't cleaned my own bathroom in years, let alone one shared by forty guys. One day, about a week and a half into my stay, I was cleaning a filthy toilet in one of the bathroom stalls. Chills ran through my body, and a cold sweat dripped off me as the smell of feces and industrial cleaning detergent made me gag while I scrubbed. I sat on the toilet, exhausted, frustrated, and overwhelmed, and then started to cry.

The prayer was quick and not at all eloquent: 'I can't do this, God. I don't have the strength or willpower.'"

REFLECTION

One of the most powerful images in Scripture is Jesus, the Son of God, Creator of heaven and earth, kneeling to wash the feet of His disciples.

Jesus teaches in Mark 9:35, *"If anyone would be first, he must be last of all and servant of all."*

Many of us think miracles look like crashing thunder or parted seas. But sometimes the real miracle looks like scrubbing toilets with a surrendered heart.

My job at Keswick was not glamorous. At times it was grueling. But God had a purpose in it. Something powerful was happening as I knelt in that filthy bathroom stall. While I was busy scrubbing toilets, the Holy Spirit was scrubbing my heart. Through sweat, surrender, and desperation, He was shaping me into a disciple.

One of my favorite passages is Proverbs 3:5–6. It is also one of the hardest to live out. We are told to trust in the Lord with all our heart, to lean not on our own understanding, and in all our ways to acknowledge Him, trusting that He will direct our paths. God's plan is often counterintuitive. We are not always going to understand it. But it is always worthy of our trust. As my old pastor and mentor in the faith, Bill Beckleman, once told me, "There is nothing more profound than the mind of God."

Faithfulness is not always flashy. It is often hidden in service, obscured by stench, and soaked in prayer. This is where Jesus meets us. Whispered prayers under our breath. Too tired to polish them before they leave our lips.

He who is lifted up in spirit by success
is often brought low by humble service.
— Gregory the Great

CHRIST IN THE DARKNESS

"Peace be with you. As the Father has sent me,
even so I am sending you."
—John 20:21, ESV

PRAYER

Jesus, I don't always have the strength. But You do. Teach me to find You in the mundane, the messy, and the overlooked. Make me faithful in the small things. Let my labor become worship. And scrub my heart clean again.

In Jesus' name, Amen.

SELAH

A moment to pause and reflect

Pause and notice.

What lingered after the reading ended?

Where did you feel resistance or hesitation?

What might God be inviting you to trust even without clarity?

Sit quietly. Let your thoughts settle.

JOURNAL

The Altar and the Impossible
When Love Redeems

EXCERPT FROM *HE CALLS ME REDEEMED*

"Standing at that altar with Nicole brought my life completely into focus. I saw her, really saw her, for exactly who she was—that girl standing alone in the bar, alone just like I was, scared and disappointed, always looking for love but never finding it—and all I wanted to do was protect her and provide for her. To love her. I had never been more sure of anything in my life...

It doesn't happen every day that a narcotics officer gives his daughter away to a guy with my history, but that is the kind of impossible thing God does. I was grateful for his blessing and the trust he put in me that day, knowing my past and trusting me to love her."

REFLECTION

I had never seen anything so beautiful as my wife as she walked down the aisle, her white gown gathered gently at the waist before cascading into flowing layers that moved with each step, like a quiet tide of lace and light. But it was the way she looked at me that made the whole world disappear behind her.

Redemption doesn't just change your habits. It transforms your heart. This moment at the altar wasn't about marriage alone. It was about mission. About being trusted. About being seen not for who I had been, but for who I had become.

Love can be terrifying after abuse, addiction, or major trauma. Intimacy feels risky. Vulnerability feels dangerous. But God is in the restoration business. He doesn't just heal you for yourself. He heals you so you can love, protect, and build with someone else.

That altar marked the beginning of a new story. One only God could write. It began with what once felt impossible: a father, a narcotics officer, placing his daughter's hand into mine. A man redeemed from a life of crime being entrusted with something so precious. That is grace. That is trust. Those are the fingerprints of the Savior.

It is not your love that sustains the marriage, but from now on, the marriage that sustains your love. In your love you see only the heaven of your own happiness, but in marriage you are placed at a post of responsibility toward the world and mankind. Love is your own private possession, but marriage is more than something personal. It is a status, an office.
— Dietrich Bonhoeffer

CHRIST IN THE DARKNESS

"Simon, son of John, do you love me?" He said to him, "Yes, Lord; you know that I love you." He said to him, "Feed my sheep."
—John 21:16, ESV

PRAYER

Jesus, thank You for the gift of love. Thank You for making me someone who can be trusted again. Help me love well and serve well as my faith matures in You. Teach me to put others above myself and to serve You above all else.

In Jesus' name, Amen.

SELAH

A moment to pause and reflect

Take a gentle breath.

Allow the words to remain without explanation.

What stirred within you?

Where did you sense both grief and grace?

How might God be meeting you beneath the surface?

Remain still for a moment.

Legacy in the Living Room
The Father's Love

EXCERPT FROM *HE CALLS ME REDEEMED*

"By this time, I was basking in the glory of being a new father. After a lifetime of dreaming about it, I had finally become a daddy. Some of the greatest gifts I have are pictures of my grandfather holding my son Arman, his great-grandson. As my son entered into this world, my grandfather was exiting it...

I looked in through the storm door at my son crawling around on the floor and thought about what kind of man he would be. Then I walked back in and did my best to come up with just the right words to explain to my grandfather how God wanted his heart.

He looked at me and said, 'Not only my heart, but my mind and my soul as well.'"

REFLECTION

Some stories end in loss. Others begin with it. Mine held both at once: my grandfather on his way out, my son Arman on his way in, and me standing in the middle. Living a life I never thought possible.

This is the miracle of generational redemption. God did not just save me. He made me a father. He gave me something to pass on. Not a legacy of silence, addiction, and pain, but a legacy of faith, hope, and love.

There I was, looking through the storm door at my son crawling across the living room floor, while inside my grandfather prepared to meet the Lord. One generation fading. Another just beginning. And in between them stood a man who once should have been dead, now speaking about Christ.

That living room became holy ground. Not because of anything dramatic, but because God was weaving a story across generations.

I am not just a survivor of what almost destroyed me. I am a steward of what God restored.

Redemption does not stop with one life. It moves through families. It rewrites what gets handed down.

Let everything take second place to our care of our children, our bringing them up to the discipline and instruction of the Lord. If from the beginning he learns to be a lover of wisdom, he will have riches greater than all riches, and greater glory.
— John Chrysostom

Christ in the Darkness

"But you will receive power when the Holy Spirit has come upon you, and you will be my witnesses in Jerusalem and in all Judea and Samaria, and to the end of the earth."
—Acts 1:8, ESV

Prayer

Father, thank You for the gift of family, for the ones who came before me and the ones I now get to raise. Let me be a man who passes down faith. Let my children see Christ in me. Let what I hand them be healing, hope, and truth.

In Jesus' name, Amen.

SELAH

A moment to pause and reflect

Slow down.

Let today's reflection echo softly.

What felt closest to your own experience?

Where do you feel tension between fear and faith?

What might it look like to stay present with God here?

Speak openly. Listen quietly.

There Is Hope
The Final Invitation

EXCERPT FROM *HE CALLS ME REDEEMED*

"Whoever you are, wherever you are, and whatever you've done, there is hope for you in Jesus Christ. Forgiveness for you, rest for you, in Jesus Christ. You can be forgiven and have peace with God today, right here as you read this, through Jesus if you will believe in your heart and confess with your mouth that He is Lord, and that He is who He says He is. He will come into your heart and change your life for all eternity...

My hope and my prayer and what I'd love most is if you would honestly examine your life and your heart and ask yourself the hard questions. I'd love it if you would hear the Gospel—the good news—through my book, get alone with God, and have a moment like I did all those years ago when I was hopeless and ready to give up on life."

REFLECTION

Our journey together began in darkness. But it ends with an invitation. Throughout these pages, I have written from a place of pain, sorrow, shame, and loss. I have traced what it means to cry out from the pit and to encounter a God who does not turn away from that cry. The same God who met the psalmist in Psalm 88 met me in my darkest hour and transformed my life forever.

This is the heart of the gospel in two words:

Come home.

No matter where you've been. No matter what you've done. Jesus Christ offers forgiveness, rest, and peace, not someday, but today.

This is not an ending. It is an open door. An invitation. One prayer away.

CHRIST IN THE DARKNESS

*"I am the resurrection and the life.
Whoever believes in me, though he die, yet shall he live."*
—John 11:25, ESV

PRAYER

Jesus, I want to know You. I believe You are who You say You are. Forgive me. Heal me. Save me. Make me new. I give You my heart, my past, my future, everything. Thank You for meeting me in the dark. From this day on, I will follow You.

In Jesus' name, Amen.

SELAH

Pause and rest.

Allow the journey of these days to settle.

What has changed in your heart?

Where do you see growth, even if small?

What would you say to God now that you could not say before?

Remain still. Let silence become prayer.

You have come through thirty days of honesty, prayer, and fragile hope.

You have cried out from the depths, walked through shadows, and poured

out your soul before God.

This moment is not an ending.

It is a threshold.

You are not who you were when you began this journey. Something has

shifted. Words have been spoken that once felt impossible to pray. Silence

has been endured. Truth has surfaced.

Wisdom has been given. Access has been granted.

And if you have never fully surrendered your life to Jesus Christ, let this be

the moment you do not turn away from what has been stirring in you.

JOURNAL

"He who is the blessed and only Sovereign, the King of kings and Lord of lords, who alone has immortality, who dwells in unapproachable light, whom no one has ever seen or can see. To him be honor and eternal dominion. Amen."

— 1 Timothy 6:15–16 (ESV)

The Gospel of Jesus Christ

God created you for relationship with Him. But sin fractures that relationship, leaving us searching for life where it cannot be found. No amount of effort, self-improvement, or religion can heal that separation.

So God came to us.

Jesus Christ entered our darkness. He lived the life we could not live, bore the weight we could not carry, and died the death we deserved. He rose again to offer forgiveness, freedom, and new life.

"But God shows his love for us in
that while we were still sinners, Christ died for us."
— Romans 5:8 (ESV)

Jesus did not come for the self-sufficient.

He came for the weary.

The addicted.

The ashamed.

The broken.

He came for you.

"Everyone who calls on the name of the Lord will be saved."
— Romans 10:13 (ESV)

If you are ready to respond, you can pray in your own words,
or simply pray something like this:

A Prayer of Surrender

Jesus,

I need You.

I believe You died for me and rose again.

I repent of my sin.

Forgive me. Heal me. Change me.

I give You my life completely.

Amen.

If you prayed that prayer, or if God met you in a new way through these pages, do not walk forward alone. Tell someone. Seek out a Bible-teaching church. Continue in prayer and Scripture.

This is not the end of the story.

It is only the beginning.

If this book met you in the dark,
would you take a moment to share it?

Your review helps this message reach someone else
who may be there right now.

Scan here to leave a review.

If this book has met you in a meaningful way, I invite you to continue the journey.

HE CALLS ME REDEEMED

A memoir of childhood sexual abuse, heroin addiction, hope, and redemption.

This devotional was born from that story. If you would like to read the full testimony behind these pages, you can find He Calls Me Redeemed wherever books are sold. You can also explore additional writing, resources, and updates at:

WWW.ARMANKAYMAKCIAN.COM

You can also connect with me on social media.

If this book encouraged you, consider leaving a review online. Thoughtful reviews help other readers discover books like this and matter more than you know.

Arman Kaymakcian is available for speaking engagements, panel discussions, and interviews on topics including faith and suffering, addiction and recovery, childhood trauma, redemption, and the hope of the gospel.

To partner with your church, school, hospital, rehabilitation facility, or correctional institution, or to inquire about bulk orders or television, radio, or podcast appearances, please contact: akaymakcian@gmail.com

Thank you for reading.

Thank you for walking through the dark with me.

May you remember that even in the darkest places,
you are never alone.

Arman Kaymakcian

Acknowledgments

First, I thank my Lord and Savior, Jesus Christ, whose mercy did not abandon me in the darkest hours of my life and whose faithfulness continues to sustain me.

To my beautiful wife, Nicole, and my incredible sons, Arman, Nikos, and Theo: thank you for your unwavering love and support. You have made sacrifices so that I might serve God through my writing, and I am deeply grateful for each of you. You have been, and will always be, the most important part of my life. I pray that these words may be a comfort to you and your children and grandchildren for many years to come. Any success I experience belongs to you as well. You are the greatest thing that's ever happened to me. I love you more than words can express. This book belongs to you.

A special thank you to my pastor, my friend, and my brother, Chris Durkin, for writing the foreword for He Meets Us in the Dark. And to his wife, Melissa, and his children—Ethan, Abigail, JJ, Liam, Annabel, and Charlie—thank you for the constant encouragement and spiritual investment in my family and I. Thank you for the wisdom and wit, for your patience and prayers, and for your dedication and devotion to your family, my family, and the entire family of God.

To Pastor Jacob Navey, and his wife, Hayley, and their children—Eli, Canaan, and Selah—thank you for your friendship and sincerity, for your love and dedication to God's house, for coffee and countless early mornings, and for powerful prayers and thoughtful conversations about theology. Thank you for your faithfulness and friendship.

I thank God for the countless spiritual mentors and companions in Christ who have helped guide me throughout the years. I could write many pages of names, but I would like to take this opportunity to name a few people from my time as a brand-new believer who walked with me through some of the most difficult and pressing times of my life, and whom the Lord especially used to begin smoothing out my many rough edges.

Chaplain Jim Freed, who has gone to be with the Lord, who was used by God to call me out of darkness and into the light. He met me at the very threshold of my faith in Christ and at the beginning of my walk with the Lord. I will never forget the way he dropped to his knees in the mud to pray with me at some of the weakest moments of my life.

To Pastor Bill Beckleman and his wife, Candace: thank you for your agape love, for your poise and patience, for your prayers, and for your unwavering commitment to proclaiming the gospel. Your faithfulness to Scripture shaped far more than these pages.

To Chaplain Robert Roman: thank you for your counsel, your resilience, and your faith both in and out of the valley. You helped me heal in ways most will never comprehend.

To Rob Russamano and his wife, Terri, thank you for showing me faith through faithfulness and for shaping how I see physical work as a literal offering to God.

To those who contributed professionally to this work, including editors, designers, and early readers who offered honest critique rather than easy affirmation, thank you for helping refine what I could not always see clearly myself. Your precision strengthened this book immensely.

To every person who has entrusted me with their story of struggle, doubt, grief, addiction, or silence, your courage matters. If anything written here serves another soul walking through darkness, it is because I have witnessed your resilience and faith.

To God alone be the glory.

ARMAN KAYMAKCIAN

 is an Armenian-American writer from New Jersey with Italian roots whose work explores faith, suffering, memory, and redemption. He is the author of He Calls Me Redeemed, a memoir tracing his journey through childhood sexual abuse, heroin addiction, and a life transformed by an encounter with Jesus Christ.

Rooted in both personal testimony and the spiritual tradition of the church, his writing refuses easy answers to suffering while bearing witness to the quiet persistence of grace. His poetry has appeared in Jewel City Review and in publications of the Armenian General Benevolent Union.

Kaymakcian is also a public speaker and advocate for children's safety and addiction recovery, drawing on his own story to encourage those navigating darkness and to raise awareness about the realities of abuse and the ongoing drug epidemic.

He lives in New Jersey with his wife and three sons.

www.ingramcontent.com/pod-product-compliance
Lightning Source LLC
Chambersburg PA
CBHW031025160726
47991CB00005B/1870